OUT OF THE CITY, ACROSS THE SANDS

OUT OF THE CITY, ACROSS THE SANDS

Retracing Abraham's steps from Ur to Canaan

Paul Bork, Ph.D.

Review and Herald Publishing Association
Washington, D.C. 20012

Editor: Thomas A. Davis
Cover Design: Howard Bullard

Printed in U.S.A.

ACKNOWLEDGMENTS: Scripture quotations marked R.S.V. are from the Revised Standard Version of the Bible, copyrighted 1952, 1971 by the Division of Christian Education of the National Council of Churches of Christ in the U.S.A.

Verses marked T.L.B. are taken from *The Living Bible,* copyright 1971 by Tyndale House Publishers, Wheaton, Ill. Used by permission.

Library of Congress Cataloging in Publication Data

Bork, Paul F., 1924—
Out of the city, across the sands.

Bibliography: p.
1. Abraham (Biblical patriarch) 2. Bible. O.T. Genesis XI, 27-XXIV, 18—Criticism, interpretation, etc. 3. Bible. O.T. Genesis XI, 27-XXIV, 18—Antiquities. 4. Bible. O.T. Genesis XI, 27-XXIV, 18—Geography. I. Title.
BS580.A3B58 1982 222'.110924 82-20515

ISBN 0-8280-0207-X

Contents

Dedication

To the thousands of students
who have gone through my classes and whose
inquisitive minds have kept me searching,
this book is affectionately dedicated.

Preface

The train from Baghdad jolted to a stop at Nasiriya at 3:30 A.M. Having given up any hope of sleeping, my family and I emerged into the hot, dark night and vied with other passengers in a headlong race to the 1946 vintage taxis waiting outside the station. A frantic, bone-jarring five-minute ride deposited us at the government-operated tourist rest house to await the dawn and our long-planned visit to Ur of the Chaldees. Our quest for the birthplace of the man who was God's friend had at last begun.

Years of study and preparation had preceded this trip. Numerous seasons of archeological field research of the patriarchal age in the Middle East now served me as excellent background to the life and times of Abraham.

But why had I chosen Abraham? Why not Moses, David, Solomon, or Nebuchadnezzar, to mention a few? Moses, God's incomparable leader, had already been the object of my research; this had resulted in an earlier book, *The World of Moses.* David, Solomon, and Nebuchadnezzar were also extraordinary people and deserve careful consideration. But Abraham, whose unique story Moses also chose to write, has always been considered the greatest figure described in the Old Testament.

Although, as far as is known, Abraham never wrote a book or even a psalm, he is given more space in the patriarchal account than any other individual. Of the many centuries covered in the Genesis story, Abraham's life of about 175 years is recorded in fifteen chapters, while the combined stories of Creation, the entrance of sin, the Flood, the Tower of Babel, the dispersion of nations, and all the other preceding events, are contained in ten chapters.

Another inference of the way God felt about the importance of the life of Abraham may be drawn from Hebrews 11, the Bible's Hall of Faith. Abraham's life and experience is given more space than that of Moses and the combined accounts of all the other heroes in the chapter.

Even in today's religious world, Abraham's preeminence can be witnessed. Three of the world's major religions, comprising more than a billion adherents, claim Abraham as their physical or spiritual father—or both: Judaism, Christianity, and Islam. So there seems to be no question that we are dealing with the greatest man in Old Testament times. He was the first man in the Bible to be called a prophet.

When did Abraham live? This question has been problematic to Bible students for centuries. Some have suggested that he really didn't live at all; that his story was nothing more than a fable. Julius Wellhausen, a brilliant German scholar who died in 1918, implied that the stories of the patriarchs were a creation of a much later period and retrojected into a "hoary past." Others, who accept the account as historically possible, place it anywhere from 2000 B.C. to 1700 B.C. With the discovery of the Ebla tablets in Syria and their tantalizing parallels with the patriarchal age, it is thought that we may have to push Abraham's times as far back as 2300 B.C. Further study and translation of the tablets is needed to clarify that possibility, however.

All of these speculations arise because the Bible does not tell us precisely when Abraham was born. All that is recorded is the length of time he and other leading figures of his era lived. When we add up the years of the various generations recorded in the Bible and fit them into the historical period considered in the account, we arrive at the tentative date of the twentieth century B.C.

It is important to bear in mind that Abraham did not write his own story, nor did anyone among his contemporaries. The account was probably handed down orally from generation to generation for centuries before it was eventually included in the Genesis record.

In my earlier book, *The World of Moses,* I suggest that such information may have been kept by Jethro, Moses' father-in-law and a great Midianite prince. This is not unlikely, because the Midianites were Abraham's descendants through his wife Keturah. Moses married into this influential family after he fled from Egypt and made his home in the land of Midian. It is to this period in Midian that the Genesis record, in some form, is usually traced.

One fact always impresses itself upon me when I

associate with Bedouins of the Middle East. Many of those people who inhabit the deserts can neither read nor write, but their trained memory can recall facts and figures better than many of us can. I have heard them recite the names of twenty generations and recount facts about each of them. So it should not be surprising that in ancient times, oral tradition in all its details could be passed on from one generation to another.

Another question that arises in dealing with Abraham's life is his birthplace as already suggested. Was it Ur in southern Mesopotamia, where the Tigris and the Euphrates empty into the Persian Gulf? Or was it in northern Mesopotamia near Haran, Turkey? Persuasive arguments can be presented in favor of each location.

Those who believe Abraham's home was near Haran in northern Mesopotamia, present-day southeastern Turkey, point to the fact that several towns are known to have existed in that area in patriarchal days, some of which have names linked to Abraham, such as Serug and Nahor. The Bible also strongly implies that the area of Haran was a family base for the patriarchs. But it is not clear whether Haran became this base after Abraham's prolonged stay there on his trip from Ur to Canaan or if it was the point of his origin and departure to the Promised Land.

Although scholars are somewhat divided on the location of Biblical Ur, the majority of them favor the city near the Persian Gulf. In this book I will follow this lead.

In spite of the fact that much information has

become available to us, there is still much that remains unknown. At the rate archeology is enlightening us on the patriarchal age, we can expect a great deal more information to emerge in the near future.

CHAPTER 1

Abraham's Ancestry

These are the generations of Shem: Shem . . . Arphaxad . . . Salah . . . Eber . . . Peleg . . . Reu . . . Serug . . . Nahor . . . Terah . . . Abraham (Gen. 11:10-26).

After the Biblical flood, the descendants of Noah established themselves in the valley later known as Mesopotamia *(Meso potamia,* "between rivers"). Today the land between the Tigris and the Euphrates rivers is known as Iraq.

God's counsel to Noah and his sons that they have many children and repopulate the earth (Gen. 9:1) must have been taken seriously. The population must have truly exploded to have reached the proportions existing in Abraham's days.

The area first mentioned in the Bible where a city developed was Babylon. Here an enormous tower was built to be a monument to human ingenuity. God, whose plan was that mankind scatter over the face of the earth, rather than congregate in one place, destroyed the tower and confused the language. His plan worked—the people dispersed, moving away according to their clan or family grouping.

Noah's son Japheth took his family in the direction of Europe. Ham moved toward Palestine and Egypt. Ham's son Canaan inhabited Palestine—hence the name the Land of Canaan. Shem and his children stayed in the area of southern Mesopotamia. Here they prospered, building many towns and cities. Archeologists are generally agreed that in this area are found vestiges of the first cities of antiquity.

Another interesting similarity between the Biblical accounts and the folklore of the region is the longevity of its peoples. The Bible points out that before the Flood, human beings were living nearly a thousand years. In Ur's genealogy of kings, some of them are recorded as having ruled for periods of a thousand years before the Flood, while the average later became a reign of two hundred years, and finally less than a century.[1]

As mentioned earlier, the Semites, the descendants of Noah's son Shem, remained in the Mesopotamian valley. The line of Abraham, as given in the Bible, is listed in the following sequence: Shem, Arphaxad, Salah, Eber, Peleg, Reu, Serug, Nahor, Terah, Abraham.

Very little is known of those named between Shem and Abraham. Occasionally, it is noted that certain villages have their familiar names. Sometimes the names may be found on tablets, but there is no proof that they are necessarily those of Abraham's family.

One possible connection is Eber, the name of a king of Ebla, in northern Syria. There are some who wonder whether this may be the same Eber who was an ancestor of Abraham.

Because of the longevity of the inhabitants of this era mentioned in the Bible, several of the generations listed above lived contemporaneously. For instance, Shem lived six hundred years, and most of this period was after the Flood. Thus he spanned all the generations between himself and Abraham. As a matter of fact, he even lived for more than a century during Abraham's time. If this chronology is correct, it would be easy to visualize elderly Shem holding little Abraham on his lap, telling him stories of the Flood. In this way, Abraham could have heard the story firsthand from an eyewitness, and thus would have been able to preserve it unembellished and pass it on for future generations until it finally reached the author of Genesis.

It may be important to mention here that Flood and Creation accounts originating in the southern Mesopotamia area are, generally speaking, closer to the Biblical version than similar stories farther removed from the area. This may suggest that the stories originated here and were carried orally to other parts of the world.

Many of the Biblical details of this early period are not now, and may never be, fully substantiated as historical facts. We are dealing with events and individuals who lived about four thousand years ago. To put it in a different perspective, Abraham was as far removed *before* Christ as we are *after* Christ. It is a miracle that we are able to substantiate any part of the patriarchal age.

Less than a hundred years ago, scholars were still suggesting that the patriarchal age was little more than the product of the imagination. The influential German scholar Wellhausen, previously referred to, was prominent among these, and was a leader in the school of thought that suggested the accounts of the patriarchs were composed during Israel's monarchy (1000 B.C.), or even later, and projected back over a thousand years. But, generally speaking, this is no longer taught. In our century archeology has contributed enormously to a vindication of the historicity of the patriarchal background. We now know more about the age of Abraham than anyone has known before.

An observation by archeologist Andre Parrot illustrates how drastically archeology has changed points of view in the scholastic world: "It is difficult to deny that the Biblical accounts have been clarified and have received, in certain cases, astonishing confirmation."[2]

W. F. Albright, dean of Biblical archeologists, affirms this viewpoint: "The narratives of Genesis dealing with Abram [Abraham] may now be integrated into the life and history of the time in such surprisingly consistent ways that there can be little doubt about their substantial historicity."[3]

CHAPTER 2

Early Ur

We must revise considerably our ideas of the Hebrew patriarch when we learn that his earlier years were spent in such sophisticated surroundings; he was the citizen of a great city and inherited the traditions of an ancient and highly organized civilization.[4]

To some, a visit to the site of Ur today is disappointing. It is difficult for even the most fertile imagination to visualize that where these mute ruins stand, one of the most celebrated cities, and a center of the most prosperous and advanced culture of antiquity, existed.

Today, the location is a flat, barren desert denuded of practically all vegetation. The only living creatures seen are an occasional jackal dashing through the ruins. Even the proud Euphrates River has forsaken its former course by the city and flows at a distance of about six miles. If Abraham had lived in this area today it surely would have been no trial for him to leave his birthplace.

The Bible is silent about prepatriarchal Ur, but much information has come to light through the joint British-American archeological expedition led by Sir Leonard Woolley from 1922 to 1934. The excavation of other Middle Eastern cities has also contributed to a deeper understanding of Ur and its role in Mesopotamia.

Ur is situated some 140 miles southeast of old Babylon, and about the same distance northwest of the Persian Gulf. As my reader has already inferred, the closest town is Nasiriya, which is served by rail between Baghdad and Basrah.

When Ur was first built, it was possibly a harbor city on the Persian Gulf at the point where the Euphrates enters the sea. It is commonly believed that large amounts of silt carried by the Tigris and Euphrates rivers, accumulating over the centuries, have caused the gulf to recede to the point where today Ur is about 140 miles inland.

In the early centuries after the Flood the area of southern Mesopotamia, which became known as the land of Sumer, developed rapidly. A number of cities rose and became prominent, among which were Babylon, Erech (Uruk), and Nippur, to mention only three. The Sumerians became a powerful and influential people. Among Sumer's supreme achievements was the development of the cuneiform system of writing. The first attempt at writing was pictographic, meaning that each word or idea was expressed in the form of a picture. Thus, to convey the idea of *head,* an actual head was drawn; the word *eating* was written by a bowl and a mouth. The word *going* or *walking* was expressed by two legs in a walking position.

Later, pictures became more stylized, so that nonartists could also write. The writing tool was a stylus, a long stick like a pen with a wedge-shaped point.

In Mesopotamia, the scribes wrote on clay instead of papyrus as in Egypt, because clay was abundant in the marshy area of Ur. This material not only was easily accessible to all people but it was easy to prepare and write upon, and it was also durable. A clay tablet, properly prepared and baked, outlasts iron, copper, wood, leather, or possibly any other available material. The most commonly used writing materials, such as leather, wood, or papyrus, would have disintegrated in the dampness of southern Mesopotamia, but baked clay was not affected by the weather.

In modern times the wedge-shaped writing was given a Latin name, cuneiform, for *cuneus,* meaning "wedge." This shape was easily impressed upon moist clay, and remained sharp and easy to read after the clay was baked.

Scribal schools were developed in Ur. As the need for written communication became more and more important and necessary, scribes were in great demand. Boys were usually trained in this art and became the recorders, or secretaries. The best scribes were employed by the royal court or the temple priests. Temples were busy, enterprising institutions, as will be seen later.

Occasionally, the ruins of scribal schools have been discovered by archeologists. In the area of Ur practice tablets by the score were found, ranging from the ugliest scratches of the neophite to the beautiful forms of the best trained. Some of the professional cuneiform tablets are so clear, sharp, and well preserved that they look as though a master calligraphist had written them yesterday, instead of more than four thousand years ago. Writing was not only used to record daily routine but it soon reached a stage of development that included literary concepts and folklore.

Abraham, cultured, individual, must have known how to read and write. He may have recorded much information that he passed on to following generations, eventually reaching Moses. An example of this may be found in Genesis, where carefully detailed information suggests record keeping. It is interesting to observe this in Genesis 5 or 10, if one reads with this concept in mind. Our view of inspiration should not preclude information that was preexistent and recorded.

When Ashurbanipal was king of Assyria in the seventh century B.C., his kingdom extended to southern Mesopotamia. He secured tablets from the ancient cities of that area and had them recopied for his royal library in Nineveh. When Nineveh was burned in 612 B.C. by the Babylonians under Nabopolassar and Nebuchadnezzar, these tablets were buried under ashes, coal, and rubble, and remained there undisturbed, as if by providence, until they were excavated by archeologists during the past century.

Between the days of the Babylonians and recent times, a reading knowledge of the old cuneiform was forgotten, as was the hieroglyphics of Egypt. But in the case of both, dedicated efforts and hard work eventually unlocked these ancient forms of writing. Ancient hieroglyphics were largely decoded by a young French scholar, Jean François Champollion, aided by the Rosetta stone, in the early part of the nineteenth century.

In the case of cuneiform, much of the credit goes to a British army officer, Sir Henry C. Rawlinson, for decoding in 1846 the writings on the Behistun rock in ancient Persia, now Iran.

Darius the Great, king of Persia in the sixth century B.C., wrote some of the great achievements of his kingdom in three forms of cuneiform on the face of a granite mountain at Behistun. There it remained, through the centuries, forgotten until it came to Rawlinson's attention. Recognizing the importance of this discovery for the purpose of deciphering ancient cuneiform, Rawlinson set out to copy the entire inscription spread out over an area of more than 1,200 square feet.

To accomplish his purpose, Rawlinson had to inch his way up one hundred feet above the ground to copy hundreds of lines of trilingual cuneiform. After years of toil he not only decoded Darius' inscription but laid the foundation for reading all cuneiforms.

In this way, our reading knowledge of the ancient cuneiform of Mesopotamia came about. With this information an ancient civilization was gradually disclosed. With an understanding of the language, we are able to penetrate the darkness and obscurity that had fallen over the civilization of Abraham's time, obliterating it from our view.

As archeologists have unearthed thousands of tablets of Ur and neighboring cities of that early period, we are able to see what records these people kept, their history, their thinking, and their business projects.

Interesting, from a Biblical perspective, among the records of the Sumerians are stories that present analogies to the Scripture accounts of Flood and pre-Flood events. Tablets containing these narratives were among the royal library records of Ashurbanipal in Nineveh. Others were found in southern Mesopotamia. The tablets in existence are all copies of earlier ones, probably dating back to times before the Genesis account was written. The fact that versions of the same stories were found in many places suggests the widespread belief in them.

Seven clay tablets, totaling a little more than one thousand lines, contain a poem dealing with the creation of heaven and earth. This poem is referred to as the *Enuma Elish,* translated "When above," these being its first two words. Although many of the details in the story have no parallel with the Bible, others seem unmistakably clear in their reference to Creation.

In the *Enuma Elish* epic[5] there were three gods, two parents and a son, who set out to create the world, which came out of an undefined mass of water.

Other clay records supply more details, describing a world that at first was all water. Later in the story, land, sky, grass, trees, and animals were created. The sun and the moon were set in space for light and for regulation of time. Finally, two servants were brought into existence. "He made [them more] glorious [than a]ll [other] creatures."[6] They were made of clay, part human, part divine. The formation of man constituted the final act of

Creation.

Upon contemplation of the universe by the gods, there followed rest and celebration. The seven-day period for Creation as emphasized in the Genesis account is absent in Sumerian narratives or legends.

Some interpreters of these records see in them hints of man's fall into sin and restoration, but these are not generally accepted by scholars, so they will be left out of consideration here.[7]

Another great poem found among the tablets of Ashurbanipal's library is called the Epic of Gilgamesh, which is very close at some points to the Biblical flood story. This Sumerian account is even closer in detail to the Biblical account than their Creation story. One possible reason for this was that the Flood had occurred more recently and according to Biblical chronology, Noah's son Shem was probably still living when it was written.

We know from information on the tablets that Gilgamesh was one of the early kings of Ur's neighboring city Erech. He is thought by many to be the same person as Noah's great-grandson Nimrod, hunter, builder of cities, and king (Gen. 10:8-10). Gilgamesh is described in mythology as two thirds divine and one third mortal. He was king of Erech, a restless hero, unrivaled and undisciplined, and he tyrannized over the dwellers of his city.[8] Hittite epics ascribe gigantic proportions to him—his height being sixteen feet and his chest measurements in proportion.[9]

Gilgamesh himself was the great hero in a story in which the Flood is recounted. Here, as in the *Enuma Elish* Creation story, many parts have little resemblance to the Biblical account, but in many other areas the analogy is so close that most scholars would agree that both stories are dealing with the same event. In this narrative the reason given for the destruction of the world by a flood was that the gods were unhappy over the conditions among the inhabitants of the earth.

In another Mesopotamian flood story it is mentioned that the father god, "Enlil, in a fit of anger at the raucous behavior of humankind, destroyed everyone except Atrahasis [equivalent of Noah] and those who cohabited his ark."[10]

This is similar to the concept expressed in the Biblical record, where it is stated that "God saw that the wickedness of man was great in the earth, and that every imagination of the thoughts of his heart was only evil continually" (chap. 6:5).

In the Epic of Gilgamesh the gods apparently were not united in the decision, for one of them decided to save some living-kind. Uta-napishtim was told to build a boat so that he, his family, and many animal species could be saved. In this account, as in the Biblical story, the dimensions of the boat were supplied. It was to be a cube, the sides measuring 120 (Babylonian) cubits, or about 200 feet—a most unusual shape for a boat! Noah's ark, which was 450 feet long, 75 feet wide, and 45 feet high was, in its proportions, much more seaworthy. The cubical ark had seven stories, each divided into seven compartments. As with Noah's ark, pitch was used to make it watertight and there was also a door and a window.

The boat in the Gilgamesh account was loaded

with silver and gold, cattle and wild creatures, as well as the man's family and kin. The door of the boat was shut, and those inside waited for the water. After the rains came and the waters swelled, even the gods feared for their lives. The tempest continued for seven days.

In this story, the place where the ark rested is called Mount Nisir, which today is believed to be the Lesser Zab Basin, a region east of the Tigris.

After waiting for seven more days, Uta-napishtim released a dove to see whether it could find land, but it returned. A swallow followed, but it too came back. Finally a raven did not return.

By way of comparison, the Biblical order in which birds were sent out was raven, dove, dove. Some scholars point out that in antiquity it was customary among sailors to send out birds to reconnoiter.[11]

Finally, the boat was opened, people and animals disembarked, Uta-napishtim offered sacrifices, and the gods were gratified.

These were legends with which Abraham must have been familiar. If Shem, who was in Noah's ark, was indeed living with or near Abraham, he may have given the patriarch a true rendition of the event. He, in turn, would pass it on. The account could thus have eventually reached Moses, through whom we receive the Biblical version.

The Creation and Flood accounts are only two of many epics that were recounted among the Sumerians. Easterners have always been great storytellers, and mythological stories were concocted and propagated in great profusion.

CHAPTER 3

Ur of Abraham's Day

As an example of goldsmith's work this [helmet of beaten gold] is the most beautiful thing we have found in the cemetery, finer than the gold daggers or the heads of bulls, and if there were nothing else by which the art of these ancient Sumerians could be judged we should still, on the strength of it alone, accord them high rank in the role of civilized races.[12]

Practically nothing was known about Ur and its people a century ago. Today, this area is one of the best known of the ancient Near East, thanks almost entirely to the painstaking science of archeology.

The trophies of excavations are seen in museums, but archeology is infinitely more than digging up trophies or treasures. Sometimes a piece of broken pottery, commonly known as a shard, may be of greater importance than a piece of gold. It may tell a ceramist how the pottery was made, the century when it was created, if imported or local, the type of finish, and the paint used. Even incisions on it can have great significance.

As an illustration, consider a paleobotanist working on a dig. He can, through floatation procedures, gather ancient seeds and even pollen to determine vegetation and harvests of thousands of years ago.

Other specialists that often take part in excavations are numismatists (for the study of coins), paleontologists, zoologists, anthropologists, geologists, linguists, historians, epigraphers, as well as computer technicians, photographers, and draftsmen, to mention a few. Archeology is a highly specialized science today, and as a result it is extracting more and more sophisticated information from excavations and from the study of ancient ruins or remains. Thus, an ancient culture can be re-created to an amazing degree of detail and accuracy. Some work is done on site, but most of its conclusions are reached in the solitude of an office or laboratory after the complete picture of a dig is examined.

A number of the original urban centers in southern Mesopotamia have been excavated. Among these were Lagash, Nippur, Uruk, Eridu, Larsa, Isin and Ur, and these have contributed substantially to an overall picture. Books could be written about each of them.

In the case of Ur,[13] excavated under the direction of Sir Leonard Woolley between 1922 and 1934, a fabulous picture has emerged. It was the bustling capital of Sumer, and although it had passed its peak in the days of Abraham, it was still an important center of commerce and learning even into the twentieth century B.C.[14] This is usually referred to as the Ur III period, or Third Dynasty, taking us to 2006 B.C. The closing century of the third millennium B.C. is perhaps the most abundantly documented period in all cuneiform literature.[15]

During the Third Dynasty, Ur was the capital of a commercial empire that controlled all of Mesopotamia. Its influence was felt as far north as Anatolia (present-day Turkey) and as far west as Phoenicia (present-day Lebanon).

Since Sumer was not an abundant producer of the more valuable goods, its merchants enriched the city through international trade. Its ships sailed, by way of the Red Sea, to South Arabia, Egypt, and India, and possibly even farther.[16] Trade was also carried on by boats, or barges, on rivers and canals. But most goods were moved by donkey caravans.

Ur was probably the greatest trading city that the world knew at that time.[17] Its rich trade made it a prosperous, attractive place with a high standard of living. Its merchants imported "copper and tin, exotic foods, resinous plants and aromatic woods, fruit trees and herbs, ingredients for tanning, dyeing and cleaning, lumber and even the prized tortoise shell. In return, the royal traders were able to offer the bulkier staples that Mesopotamia produced far in excess of its own needs: wool, barley, wheat, dates, dried fish, fish oil and skins."[18]

It is thought by some archeologists that Abraham, too, was a businessman trading with caravans.[19] There is strong evidence for this, and it will be dealt with later. From the Biblical account we know that Abraham was very rich, knowledgeable about national and international law, and a skilled statesman who often associated with kings and princes. These characteristics he must have developed at Ur.

Ur was a great center of learning. Writing was

early developed there, probably growing from the necessity of record keeping in business. Business records, in the form of an elaborate system of double-entry bookkeeping, were also conceived there.[20] Thousands of tablets containing national and international business transactions have been found at Ur. These, like other tablets, come in all sizes, varying according to the amount of information needed on them. Some are as small as two inches square.

Temples were centers of strong business enterprise as well as places of worship. The Sumerians believed that the gods owned everything, so the people paid rent, and brought their tithes and gifts to the temple. Since most people were destitute of silver and gold (the currencies of those days), they would bring their contributions in kind, such as sheep, goats, barley, oil, and wool. The temple priests made receipts written on tablets for these offerings, one copy for the donor and one for the temple file.[21]

To transact the business of the temple gifts—to care for and redistribute them as wages—temples hired hundreds, perhaps thousands, of workers. These workers not only cared for the temples per se but were used as textile weavers, laborers on extensive holdings of temple property, and as vendors of goods. The concept of religious entities engaging in financial enterprises is not new.

Perhaps the greatest single physical monument to Ur's greatness in the days of Abraham was the enormous tiered structure, in part still standing today, which archeologists call a ziggurat.

Ziggurats are not peculiar to Ur. Many cities in the whole length of the Mesopotamian valley, as well as elsewhere, have similar structures. In Iran (anciently called Persia, a beautiful ziggurat of the fourteenth century B.C., called Choga Zanbil, remains to this day. It is thought that the Tower of Babel may have been such a ziggurat, perhaps a very large one. The base of what may have been that tower is still visible in Babylon. If the remains of the old tower were still standing in Nebuchadnezzar's day, they may have been destroyed by him when he rebuilt the city.

The architectural concept of the pyramids of Egypt may be similar to that of the ziggurats. The pyramids of Central America, in countries such as Mexico and Guatemala, are also sometimes thought to have a similar common beginning, at least in design and purpose.

In Egypt, the pyramids were built of stone, because that material was abundant in the region. This is equally so in Central America. In Mesopotamia, stone is rare, and bricks had to be used.

The ziggurat of Ur has the appearance of a layered cake with the largest part at the base and smaller tiers superimposing one on top of the other. Only the first and part of the second tiers remain. The measurements at the base are 200 feet by 150 feet. Three majestic stairways of one hundred steps each lead up to the higher elevations.

The bricks of which the ziggurat is made are each about twelve inches square. The bricks of which the solid inner part of the structure is made are sun dried. The outer part of the structure, about eight feet thick, is built of kiln-dried bricks. These are inscribed with the name of King Ur-Nammu. The sides have holes called weepers, or sweat holes, for drainage. Sun-dried bricks absorb moisture, and were it not for these holes, the structure would split or even burst.

The bricks were bound together with pitch, just as the Biblical account mentions in the erection of the Tower of Babel: "and they had brick for stone, and bitumen for mortar" (Gen. 11:3, R.S.V.). Apparently, so much bitumen or asphalt was used that today the local people call the structure *el-Muquayyar,* the Mound of Pitch.

Asphalt was, and still is, abundant in this oil-rich part of the world. Even today, oil oozes out of the ground in some areas of Iraq.

The part of the ziggurat at Ur that has survived after more than four thousand years suggests a grandeur of size and beauty of design that is difficult to match anywhere in the Near or Middle East. The architects who conceived and executed this gigantic masterpiece, which must have required thousands of laborers and years of work, were surely extremely capable men. The structure was built on what may have been the base of an even older ziggurat.[22]

In Egypt, the pyramids were used as monuments and tombs of the Pharaohs. In Central America they were used mostly for religious purposes; only in a few cases were they used as tombs. In Ur, no tombs seem to be included in the ziggurat; the purpose was primarily religious. The royal cemetery was beside it. The honor and glory of the ruling monarch who had it built must have also been considered, as in the case of Ur-Nammu, who ruled shortly before Abraham's time.

One wonders why such gigantic monuments—in the case of Ur there is no evidence of any other building in the area even approaching it in size—were erected on the plains of Mesopotamia. Some have suggested the fear of floods as a reason. It is true that both the Tigris and the Euphrates rivers are subject to periodic floodings and these structures could accommodate thousands of people above a flood.

When Woolley was excavating Ur, he came upon evidence of a flood of major proportions in a very early period of the city's history:

> It was a vast flood in the valley of the Tigris and the Euphrates which drowned the whole of the habitable land between the mountains and the desert.[23]

Some suggest that this is the flood spoken of in the Biblical account and in the Gilgamesh epic, but this is most unlikely.

In any case floods did occur in that area, and the inhabitants lived in fear of them. Whether the ziggurat was built to save people from a flood remains a matter of speculation.

The part that seems clear about the use of the ziggurat is its religious function. It was dedicated to Ur's patron deity, Sin, or Nanna, that is, the moon. This heavenly body, a favorite of people of all nations, was anciently popular among the peoples of the Middle East, as it still is. A look today at the flags of the Moslem nations of this general region gives evidence of their esteem for the moon.

Without question, the most sensational find by Woolley in Ur was made during the last season of his excavation. The discovery was the royal cemetery[24] of Ur. Some of these tombs go back centuries before Abraham.

In the tombs the excavators found a quantity of the most ornate and exquisite objects lavished on the dead; the tomb floor was actually littered with these splendid art creations. Among them were such items as a dagger with a blade of gold, a handle of silver plated over wood, and a sheath of silver suspended by a silver belt; several golden lyres with mosaic inlay of white shell, a bull's head of hammered gold, with eyes of shell and lapis lazuli, projecting from the sound box; golden wig helmets, with beautifully engraved designs; golden cups, probably used by royalty; and many other objects of gold. All these suggested that the goldsmiths of Ur had few equals.

But perhaps the most unusual aspect of these enormous graves was that which is interpreted as a sacrifice of human and animal victims. Soldiers, carts and oxen, charioteers, and attendants were included in these tombs. Tomb 1,237, which Woolley calls the "death-pit," measured twenty-seven by twenty-four feet, and held six male and sixty-eight female victims. Tomb 789 held sixty-three bodies dressed in full armor. Attendants were clothed in ornate regalia of elegantly styled and bejeweled headdress; at times there were harps and lyres by their side. All these individuals were probably killed and laid in orderly rows.

CHAPTER 4

Daily Life in Ur

"The Lord God of Israel says, 'Your ancestors, including Terah the father of Abraham and Nahor, . . . worshiped other gods'" (Joshua 24:2, T.L.B.).

Life in Ur in Abraham's day must have been busy. Ur was a very large city for its time. Archeologists suggest a population between 300,000 and 500,000. There may have been few, if any, cities in Mesopotamia larger than this one.

Since Ur depended largely on inner-city and international commerce for its prosperity, many of its citizens engaged in buying, selling, organizing caravans, and supplying caravan needs. This meant providing food and shelter for many thousands of donkeys and their drivers, equipping or repairing harnesses, weaving baskets in which merchandise was carried, et cetera. Caravans are frequently mentioned in tablets.

Thousands of persons worked at maintaining the roads and water canals, an excellent system which linked Ur with its neighbor cities. But sandstorms must frequently have made roads and canals impassable. This is still a serious problem in many parts of the land between the rivers today.

As we saw in the previous chapter, many individuals were employed in the temples as weavers, scribes, farmers, and many other occupations. Wages were usually paid in products. Thus, a weaver at the temple might receive goods such as oil, cheese, or wheat, brought in as tithe. Temples often had large land holdings where crops were raised. These products were sold locally or shipped abroad. Agricultural products, Ur's main export, were badly needed for balance of payments—an old problem!

Children had to learn to work early in life. Only those of the most affluent families went to school, which was neither universal or compulsory. The student's main objective was to learn to read and write. Much time was spent in taking dictation and in recitation. Cuneiform was not easy to read or to write, so the children spent long hours learning characters that in some ways resemble the Chinese pictographic form of writing. But they also studied literature, geography, astronomy, botany, zoology, and accounting. Noah Kramer, perhaps one of the greatest authorities on Sumer, points out that "the curriculum was stiff, the teaching methods drab, the discipline harsh."[25]

Schools, called tablet houses, were not large. Students grouped around a teacher rather than an institution. In a school there was the principal teacher, who was the expert and person in charge. An assistant teacher would go from student to student as a helper. He was called the school son. In some schools there was also the person in charge of attendance and discipline. The rod was not spared.

The cuneiform signs for caning were "stick" and "flesh"—very appropriate.

Hundreds of practice tablets have been found, giving much information about the schools and class subject matter. They also reveal student-teacher relationships.

One tablet shows that teachers had problems with some students. It tells the teacher's reaction to poor work done by a student. "You dolt, numbskull, school pest, you illiterate, you Sumerian ignoramus, your hand is terrible; it cannot even hold the stylus properly; it is unfit for writing and cannot take dictation."[26]

That school life was something to be feared seems clear from another tablet describing what happened when a student was late to class. " 'Why are you late?' 'Afraid and with pounding heart, I entered before my teacher and made a respectful curtsy.' "[27] It didn't help. He took canings from several teachers.

The account does not end here. At home, the boy tells what happened, so the father invites the teacher home and rewards him with some special gifts. The desired result is accomplished. The teacher leaves elated and wishes that the student may reach the pinnacle of the scribal art.[28]

Tablets not only reveal youth problems in school; they also record cases of juvenile delinquency—problems of four thousand years ago that have a very modern ring. Listen to this conversation between father and son:

"Where did you go?"

"I did not go anywhere."

"If you did not go anywhere, why do you idle about? Go to school . . . recite your assignment. . . . Come now, be a man. Don't stand about in the public square, or wander about the boulevard."

Next follows some quite revealing information that may pinpoint the reason for the student's delinquency. The father is speaking:

"I never in all my life did make you carry reeds to the canebrake. The reed rushes which the young and little carry. You, never in your life did you carry them. I never said to you, 'Follow my caravan.' I never sent you to work, to plow my field. I never sent you to work to dig up my field. I never sent you to work as a laborer.

"Others like you support their parents by working. . . . They multiplied barley for their father, maintained him in barley, oil, and wool. But you, you're a man when it comes to perverseness, but compared to them you are not a man at all."[29]

To the list of professions already alluded to, several more may be added. Benno Landsberger has compiled a list from existing Sumerian tablets: plowman, gardener, shepherd, cook, fisherman, smith, carpenter, metalworker, weaver, leather-worker, launderer, reed weaver, potter, mason, fattener of oxen, skipper, millworker, miller, perfumer, maltster (beermaker), oil presser, fowler (bird hunter), jeweler, silversmith, goldsmith, stone cutter, scribe, physician, judge, and surveyor.[30] This is not an exhaustive list, but it gives an idea of some of the occupations of Ur's inhabitants.

Medicine as practiced by the ancients is an area of interest to us today. At Sumer, as in Egypt, medicine was well on its way to becoming a profession in the days of Abraham. In Egypt, various "medical volumes" have been found dating from the time of Moses, several centuries after Abraham. These volumes, among which are the Edwin Smith Papyrus and the Papyrus Ebers, are a compilation of basic medical knowledge of those days. However, after reading them, one would hesitate to call ancient Egyptian medicine an art or a science. It was more of a hit-and-miss proposition, with some unbelievable concoctions. Since Moses also had much to say about health and preventive medicine, a comparison of the Biblical concept with the Egyptian ideas indicates divine inspiration in the Mosaic account.

In Sumer, too, we have a collection of prescriptions but not as detailed as the Egyptian counterparts. The Papyrus Ebers is 68 feet long, or a scroll of 110 pages sewn together end to end; the medical tablet found at Nippur, a city of Sumer, is only 3¾ by 6¼ inches in size and contains a dozen prescriptions. This tablet is of the century preceding Abraham. It is presently at the University Museum in Philadelphia.

Although magic and incantation were very much a part of Sumerian culture, these are not part of this medical tablet. The physician who compiled the prescriptions made up the medicine of botanical, zoological, and mineralogical sources. Sodium chloride (salt) and potassium nitrate (saltpeter) were widely used, as also were milk, snakeskin, turtle shell, and elements extracted from trees, plants, and seeds.

Medicines to be used internally were often mixed with beer to make them more palatable. If used externally, they were usually in the form of salves and filtrates. Unfortunately, our tablet does not mention the diseases for which the remedies were intended, nor is the degree of success in healing mentioned. Since the physician failed to give us quantities of the elements used in the concoction, one wonders whether this was a purposeful omission—perhaps a professional secret.

Another interesting part of life in Ur was the construction of the homes, as well as family life. Although Ur was a large and beautiful city, with stately buildings, most of the people lived in unpretentious surroundings. The ruins suggest that streets were narrow by today's standards, and that there was little city planning. The streets were crooked and wandered aimlessly. By contrast, many other cities in antiquity had a "straight street," such as the Bible describes as being in Damascus (Acts 9:11). This street was usually "Main Street."

The ruins of Ur show that the houses were often of a better-than-average appearance. In the better sections they were frequently two-story buildings constructed either of kiln-baked or sun-dried bricks. Windows were rare, and walls were plastered and whitewashed. A number of larger homes that were excavated had from ten to fourteen rooms. In the poorer section, houses were small and usually built in groups with doors opening to a common court.

The furnishings were simple: a table, chairs, skin rugs (or mats of reeds), and wooden beds. The kitchen had a wood stove, very much unlike today's stoves, and vessels of clay, stone, copper or bronze.

The food consisted mainly of bread made from wheat or barley. Dates, lentils, peas, and olives also were apparently abundant, as were such vegetables as cucumbers, garlic, cress, turnips, and lettuces. Milk derivatives, such as yogurt and cheese, were common, as were flesh and fish. Fruit was also abundant; wine, beer, honey, and oil were available to all.

Money as we know it did not exist in Ur. Coins did not come into wide usage until about the seventh century B.C. "Money" at Ur was usually silver or, at times, grain.

The prices of a few items might give us an idea of value: "An orchard of date palms was worth one shekel (about one-quarter of an ounce) of silver per sar (116 square feet); a male slave cost about eleven shekels, an ass about five gur of barley (700 quarts); a pig, two gur (about 300 quarts)."[31]

It is possible to understand some things about Abraham's home, and incidents that happened there, by knowing something of the culture of Ur that influenced those incidents. The Sumerian family was a closely knit unit. This is demonstrated throughout the Bible, and is still the way of life in much of the Middle East. Marriage was arranged by the parents, a price for the bride was set by her father, and the details of the transaction were witnessed to and recorded on a tablet. The dowry became the property of the woman, to be kept by her. The Sumerian woman had certain inalienable rights, such as holding property, controlling her own slaves, acting as a witness in legal matters, and engaging in business of her own. If she could not bear children, her husband was free to marry another woman, though she would remain his first, legal wife. If he divorced her, her dowry would remain her property and be her security. Women were often priestesses and even high priestesses.

Children were loved and cherished, and were under the absolute authority of both parents. As is evidenced by certain cases recorded in the Bible, parents could disinherit their children and sell them in payment for a debt or as slaves.

In case of death in the family, the deceased was usually buried in a cemetery, though at times burial would take place beneath the floor of the home. Burying members of the family, especially children, in this way was a widespread practice among peoples not only of the Middle East but even as far away as Mexico in pre-Columbian cultures.[32] It is not unusual to find a large clay vessel with the remains of a child in the floor of a kitchen or other room in the house. The thought may have been that in burying him there, the loved one would remain in spirit close to the family.

Religion had a prominent place in Sumerian culture. It was politheistic in nature, the pantheon in some cases having as many as some fifteen thousand gods.[33] The Bible mentions that Abraham's father, Terah, "served other gods" (Joshua 24:2).

There were religious festivals weekly, biweekly, monthly, and yearly. These festivals were often devoted to the worship of certain gods, foremost among whom was Nanna-Sin, the moon god, to whom Ur's ziggurat was dedicated. On these occasions the celebrations were held at the ziggurat and its temple. They included ceremonies to which people flocked in their "Sunday best." Paintings of scenes of these ceremonies showing the adherents and their dresses were found preserved, as well as actual remains in the royal cemetery of Ur.

Let me try to describe how a woman appeared in ceremonial procession, since that was when she wore her most beautiful clothes.

She would be wearing makeup, rouge, and eye shadow, applied with the use of a polished brass mirror. She wore large, gold, crescent-shaped earrings and her hair was beautifully styled and held in place by a large Spanish-type pin. She also wore golden leaves on her head, arranged like a crown. Several necklaces of gold, beads, and lapis lazuli were around her neck. Ornate armbands and various rings adorned wrists and fingers. Her flowing dress, reaching down to the ankle, covered one shoulder, leaving the other bare. In many instances the dress would be multicolored in vertical stripes of red and yellow, and occasionally one or two other colors.

The ceremonies in which this woman participated often called for impressive parades in which the gods were carried and exhibited. Musicians played instruments and sang hymns. Special offerings of food, animals, water, wine, beer, and incense were presented to the gods.[34]

No doubt the incense was imported from the land of Sheba (modern Yemen), a land made famous a thousand years later by its queen who visited King Solomon. In Abraham's world, Sheba was famous for its incense. The incense was valued mainly as a perfume and also as a religious symbol. Some four hundred years after Abraham, Queen Hatshepsut of Egypt sent a flotilla of nine ships to this land of incense to bring back an abundance of her favorite perfume. She even tried to transplant the sacred incense trees to her mortuary-temple at Deir el-Bahri in the Valley of the Queens. This incident was of such importance to her that she had it inscribed on the walls of her temple.

In addition to Nanna-Sin, two other gods of ancient Ur especially significant to Bible students were Dumuzi and Inanna. Dumuzi, the god of pastures and flocks, died annually and was brought back to life by his wife, Inanna. The celebration of this event became widespread in the ancient world. Some fourteen hundred years after Abraham, in Ezekiel's time, the feast was even celebrated in Judah. This is indicated by the prophet speaking of women in his country weeping for Dumuzi or Tammuz (Eze. 8:14). Apparently Tammuz became so popular among the Jews while they were in Babylonian captivity that when they adopted the calendar of that country, they also adopted the name Tammuz for one of the Jewish months.

Tammuz was the male god of fertility.[35] As already mentioned, his wife was Inanna, but she is sometimes called his sister. Inanna is better known by her Babylonian name, Ishtar, the most popular goddess of fertility, love, and war. Her circle of popularity was so wide that it reached to the Canaanites and to Israel, where she was known by the Biblical name Ashtoreth.

The Sumerians had a trinity in their pantheon: An, the sky god; Enlil, the lord of the earth; and Enki, the god of the oceans. To these was added Ishtar as the "lady of heaven,"[36] or the "Queen of Heaven."[37] The Tammuz-Ishtar combination became a pattern to be found in many cultures other than Sumerian for centuries to come. In Egypt, it was the Osiris-Isis; in Greece, Adonis-Aphrodite; and in Canaan, Baal-Ashtoreth.[38]

It is not known to what extent Abraham's relatives participated in Sumerian religion and idolatry. However, it is clear from the Bible that Abraham's father, Terah, and his brother Nahor, did serve other gods (Joshua 24:2). Since the religions of Ur and Haran were similar, Sin, the moon god, was the patron of both. Therefore, it can be understood why Haran may have been chosen by Terah as the city in which to remain for the rest of his life. When in a foreign land, people tend to search out those of like faith; it adds to a source of security and happiness. All of this was part of the heritage of Abraham.

CHAPTER 5

Political Situation at Ur—2000 B.C.

"We must consider him [Abraham] a man of refined tastes, the product of a sophisticated, civilized society. We know now that he came from a highly civilized city, which possessed a culture that compares well with our own."—Siegfried H. Horn, The Spade Confirms the Book *(1980), p. 74.*

In Abraham's time Ur, although prosperous, was restless and insecure. The political fortunes of Sumeria were shifting and unstable.

It is never wise to stake one's reputation on pinpointing events or dates that took place four thousand years ago. Every so often, new information comes to light, altering what was thought to be firm. Nevertheless, the picture of Ur that emerges with the dawn of the twentieth century B.C. is one of movement of nations from the west and from the east.

The powerful Third Dynasty of Ur came to an end in 2006 B.C., shortly before Abraham's days. With it came the end of Sumer as a "distinct political entity." [39] This was not a sudden cultural change, but a gradual one, taking place over a period of several decades.

As scholars are able to piece this period together, a West Semitic people, sometimes called Amorites (Amurru), from Palestine and Syria, peacefully infiltrated Sumer and, over a period of about two centuries, established themselves in power. Some archeologists suggest that Abraham's family was Amorite (Amorites were Semites) and was part of this movement.[40]

At one point, the Sumerians tried to stem the flow of Amorites by building a wall 175 miles long on their northwestern frontier. This is reminiscent of China's fifteen-hundred-mile-long Great Wall built 1700 years later to stop barbarian invasions. About the same time as Sumer, Egypt also was suffering a similar experience from the Amorites, and they too built a wall, one hundred miles long, to stop them.[41]

The Amorites apparently were not the only invading people. From the east (Persia, or Iran), the Elamites also invaded Ur in not-so-peaceful a manner, sacking the city.

Woolley points out that his excavation revealed that "there is not a single building of the Third Dynasty but bears the marks of violent overthrow." [42]

One problem with a modern ring is that during this period inflation festered in Ur. Tablets show that prices of barley and fish skyrocketed, selling for fifty to sixty times the normal price.[43]

The purpose of the Elamite invasion is not clear at this point. They soon left and the Amorites remained, holding the reins of government for nearly fifteen hundred years.[44]

In spite of all the ravages of war and the cultural

changes Ur experienced, it still remained a glorious and prosperous city. This was the city Abraham was asked to leave.

CHAPTER 6

Abraham's Departure From Ur

And Terah took Abram his son, and Lot the son of Haran his son's son, and Sarai his daughter in law, his son Abram's wife; and they went forth with them from Ur of the Chaldees, to go into the land of Canaan (Gen. 11:31).

It may not have been easy for Terah, Abraham, Sarai, and Lot, who lived in the beautiful and prosperous city of Ur, to leave it in exchange for a much inferior place without culture and without fame.

We do not know how many people and animals, or how much wealth, were to be part of the caravan to leave Ur. At this point Abraham, as well as Terah, may already have been wealthy and their possessions substantial.

To prepare for a trip of hundreds of miles, such as was contemplated, took careful planning. Many tablets have been found that give details about caravans. The beasts of burden had to be selected from several kinds of those best suited for the purpose. Most caravans were made up of hundreds of donkeys, each capable of bearing a load from 150 to 200 pounds. The loads had to be distributed and a record kept. Servants essential for the trip had to be chosen. Additional ones were probably acquired; others were sold, exchanged, or given freedom.

The Bible records the number of people and animals in one large caravan of Jews returning from Babylon to Jerusalem: 42,360 Jews; 7,377 servants; 736 horses; 245 mules; 435 camels; 6,720 asses (Neh. 7:66-69).

Besides the family, servants, and donkeys, there were the "drivers," the men to drive and care for the caravan. Then there was the "food on the hoof." No doubt hundreds or even thousands of sheep and goats were taken along to provide food such as milk, cheese, and yogurt, and to be killed for meat.

Probably the most important person in any caravan was the caravan leader, who would know the road, geographical features, depth of brooks to be forded, the nature of the people, tribal customs, caravan stops where shelter and water could be found, and a hundred other essential details.[45] Fighting men, to defend the caravan from an enemy attack, were also important. During a period when Abraham was already in Canaan, the Bible mentions that he had 318 men of war (Gen. 14:14). The passage describes how he used them to release Lot and his family, who had fallen prey to an invading army. These fighting men had to be carefully trained in the art of warfare.

Soldiers could also be hired to protect caravans. Attacks upon caravans were not uncommon then, and some have been recorded.[46]

A caravansary, a stopping place for caravans, could be found every so often on main roads, and were the equivalent of our motels or truck stops.

Here people could find protection, shelter, food, and water for themselves and animals—for a price, of course. These were usually one- or two-story buildings, with rooms attached one to the other, much like today's motels. The whole structure was often built around an open courtyard. Entrance was through a single wooden gate that would be kept locked at night to bar intruders.

Caravansaries are still a common sight in many countries, and occasionally play useful, but often unconventional, roles. At Ankara, Turkey's capital, a caravansary has been artistically restored to house one of the most beautiful archeological museums in existence, and is well worth seeing. On the way to Canaan, Terah and his family decided to journey from Ur toward Haran, a distance of about six hundred miles. The total journey to Canaan this way would be more than a thousand miles.

A look at a map of this region may quickly suggest the question: why not go in a direct line from Ur to Canaan, and thus save several hundred miles? The reason is simple, and Abraham knew it—the Arabian Desert. Until recent years, there were no paved roads through this desert, and only specially equipped trucks could make the journey, following desert trails. In the desert, water and food are rarely available, for animal or man. The sun beats down unmercifully, and frequently sandstorms not only obliterate the sky but completely change the configuration of the landscape. Worst of all, sharp sand, driven up by scorching winds, can destroy, cutting and tearing things almost to shreds.

So the trip through this desert for Abraham and

his caravan would almost certainly have ended in total disaster. Thus Abraham's caravan, as well as others, had to take the long way around the Fertile Crescent, adding hundreds of miles to the journey.

The Bible does not mention the route Abraham and his caravan took. All it says is that they left Ur and arrived at Haran (Gen. 11:31). Some of the busiest and most profitable caravan routes in the Middle East passed through the Mesopotamian valley. Two of the main routes followed the Tigris and the Euphrates. Each route linked up thriving cities along the way, blooming because of the caravan traffic.

The most likely route for Abraham to take was along the Euphrates. Here there was plenty of vegetation as well as fresh water, items extremely essential for a caravan like his. They would also find caravansaries and many towns and major cities, such as Larsa, Erech, Babylon, and Mari.

Caravans usually traveled by day and stopped overnight. At the end of the day, a meal was prepared over fires. Animals were slaughtered and the flesh roasted. Cows and goats were milked, and milk and flour were mixed in the preparation of dough. The dough was spread out in the shape of pizza and baked on a sheet of metal placed over the fire. Bread was eaten with cheese, meat, any vegetables available, dates, honey, parched corn, or milk. Usually, enough bread was baked for breakfast and for any other meal until the next evening. Leftover milk was placed in a skin container and made into yogurt.

Haran, the destination Abraham and his caravan

were bound for, was to northern Mesopotamia what Ur was to southern Mesopotamia—a major center of commerce and a trunk for caravan traffic. It may have taken the caravan a month or longer to reach Haran.

Although we do not know which route Abraham took, we have suggested it was the Euphrates, which was the shortest route. So let us briefly visit some of the major cities on that route.

Erech (modern Warka) was only forty miles upstream from Ur—perhaps a two- or three-day trip. This was another prosperous city, perhaps even older than Ur. Erech claimed to have had Gilgamesh as king. The Bible tells us Erech was part of Noah's great-grandson Nimrod's kingdom (chap. 10:10). The epic of Gilgamesh, in which the Flood story is recounted, was probably created here.

The people of Erech "enjoyed a free use of metal and were skilled workers in copper, and they made their pottery not by hand but on the potter's wheel."[47]

The first attempts at writing were discovered in this Sumerian city. It is indeed a great city, worth stopping by—if only to see it and then say goodbye.

After Abraham's caravan had traveled perhaps two weeks, covering some 150 miles, they came to the outskirts of the old city of Babylon. This was a city everyone remembered, for according to the story, God showed His disapproval of the motives of the tower builders by confusing their language. The result was the great dispersion.

The original site has been excavated by several archeological expeditions over a number of years.

But one looks in vain for clues to the grandeur of old Babylon. Whatever it was, it isn't there anymore, because some thirteen hundred years later, a great young king tore down the old landmarks and built a new city. Nebuchadnezzar was that king.

But Abraham must have seen it! How one wishes he had recorded what he saw.

The Amorites who invaded Ur also established themselves in Babylon. About two centuries after Abraham, a great Amorite king ruled Babylon and became immortalized in history for what is known as the code of Hammurabi, a code of laws unsurpassed by any human lawgiver until the time of the Romans. A copy of this code stands in stone in the Louvre in Paris today.

About 250 miles upstream from Babylon, Abraham came to another great cultural and commercial center, Mari, the chief city of the middle Euphrates. It was one of the principal centers of Mesopotamia during the third and early second millenniums B.C.[48] The excavation of Mari has been done by the French under the direction of André Parrot over a period of thirty years.

One of the main archeological finds of this site was the royal palace. Though of a slightly later period than that of Abraham, the palace still represented the glories of one of the city's periods of prosperity.

The palace complex was built over an area of nine acres and had no less than three hundred rooms. In spite of the passing of nearly four thousand years, some of the multicolored wall paintings of the throne room vividly revealed scenes of Mari's glorious past.

The structure contained banquet halls where hundreds of guests could be entertained and served from spacious kitchens. Even such mundane items as cake molds with fancy designs were found.

Perhaps the most significant find, from a historical and Biblical point of view, were the royal archives, containing more than twenty thousand tablets in cuneiform script. These tablets "provide the earliest insight into the complexities of suzerain-vassal relationships, diplomatic protocol, and the fluctuating alliances and plots rampant in the ancient Near East."[49]

The tablets also reveal a close relationship between the culture and customs of Mari and those of the future nation of Israel. The languages had close parallels, the names of deities, such as Yahweh, were similar; tribal names, such as Levi and Benjamin, were common in both. Such customs as awarding a double portion of inheritance to the oldest son, tribal leadership, and tribal heritage, as well as judgeship and covenant formulation, were much alike.[50]

There were also close affinities between Mari and Ur. Members of the royal families intermarried at times. The moon god, Sin, was also revered at Mari, and both cities had large ziggurats as part of the temple complex.

Mari may have been a major stop for Abraham's caravan. Perhaps he spent time talking to caravaneers coming from Canaan. He may have pondered whether to proceed upriver toward Haran or to save several hundred miles of travel by cutting across from Mari to Homs in Syria, north of Canaan. He was probably tired from the long previous stretch, and it may have been a real temptation.

It is a little more than two hundred miles from Mari to Homs, about the same distance as from Mari to Haran. The route skirts the northern fringes of the Arabian Desert. But it is still desert, with little water and vegetation, and frequent dust storms. Nevertheless, some caravans ventured to take that route.

Almost a thousand years later, when Solomon was at the height of his power and his kingdom extended to the Euphrates, he built a fortress and a tax-collection post at Tadmor, at a mountain pass. Caravan traffic between Mesopotamia and Syria had to stop there.

Taxes, which had to be absorbed by the purchaser of the transported goods, were usually paid at the crossing of each national border. Merchandise taken across a number of borders could easily double in price.

During the Greek period, the fourth and third centuries B.C., Tadmor meaning "palm tree," changed its name to Palmyra. The city reached its zenith in the Roman period. Its beautiful ruins, extremely well preserved, still stand as a mute witness to this desert city.

If Abraham pondered this cutoff at all, he decided against it, and soon the caravan was on the last leg of the journey toward Haran. Scholars point up such closeness between Mari and Haran that they often speak of the latter city as being on the horizon of Mari—in spite of a distance of about two hundred miles.

CHAPTER 7

Haran

As Edouard Dhorme has written, "It is obvious that the cult of Haran was simply a replica of that of Ur." Thus both geography and religion are in perfect agreement as to why a group departing from Ur should arrive at Haran.[51]

After a long tiresome journey of some six hundred miles, Abraham finally drew near the city of Haran. Although it was a flourishing community,[52] Haran was not known for its grandeur—there may never have been any. Its good fortune lay in its situation on a strategic crossroads of four thousand years ago.

The name *Haran* has been translated variously as "street," "highway," or "caravan town." It should actually be pronounced "Charran" (with a guttural "ch") and should not be confused with Abraham's brother's name, Haran ("Aran"). Roads from Asia Minor, Egypt, Syria, and Babylon crossed here. Caravan traffic brought wealth and fame to this city from as far away as India and possibly China, over the Silk Road.

Haran is on one of the major tributaries of the Euphrates, the Balikh River. A town, built over the earlier city, still stands there. In spite of its currently predominant Arab population, it is part of southeastern Turkey. It is hard to imagine what Haran may have looked like in ancient times. Because the site is inhabited, no major excavations have taken place, except to verify its ancient past.

The most impressive ruin is a mosque that, according to archeological evidence, was probably built over the site of an ancient temple.[53] Haran, like Ur and Mari, had a temple dedicated to the moon god Sin, thus showing a cultic relationship between each.

Although smaller than it was four thousand years ago and destitute of caravan traffic, Haran may not have looked much different than it does today, except that the crescent of Sin has become the crescent of Islam.[54] A few thousand people live here in their beehive-shaped houses. The patriarchal tradition is still strong. Any child can tell you that "Ibrahim Khalil" ("the friend Abraham") lived here.

The names of Abraham and his ancestors were names of towns around Haran. Terah was a town known as Turakhi, Nahor as Nachur, Serug was Sarugi, a town west of Haran. Phaliga, a town on the Euphrates, is reminiscent of Peleg.[55]

The area around Haran was known as Paddan-aram (Gen. 25:20, R.S.V.), meaning "field of Aram." At a later period we have the expression "Aramean highway" used.[56] Abraham and his posterity became so closely associated with the people of this area that they came to be known as "Arameans" (Deut. 26:5, R.S.V.). Arameans were, and still are, clever business people.

Terah and his family decided to stay at Haran,

perhaps because of its lucrative possibilities. It is also possible that for old father Terah, the six-hundred-mile journey from Ur was enough travel. In any case, the family stayed here until Terah's death at age 205 (Gen. 11:32); then, following God's call, Abraham and his family, and Lot, continued on their journey toward Canaan. Nahor, Abraham's brother, stayed at Haran, and through him and his descendants a patriarchal tradition continued in that area (chaps. 11:31, 32; 12:4, 5).

Long years later, in Canaan, after his son Isaac was 40 years old, Abraham sent his most trusted servant back to Haran to find a wife for his son. After the woman was found, the consent of her family was quickly secured, possibly in view of the large dowry Abraham had sent. The woman was Rebekah, Nahor's granddaughter.

The patriarchal ties of Haran and Canaan were renewed once more after Isaac had a son named Jacob. This son returned to Haran himself to find a wife, although virtually penniless and a fugitive. He married Leah and Rachel, daughters of Laban and great-granddaughters of Nahor. The cultural circumstances of marriage will be discussed later.

While at Haran, Jacob became a shepherd for his father-in-law, Laban. In a caravan city such as Haran, where thousands of caravaneers were continually coming and going, goats and their byproducts, milk, yogurt, cheese, flesh, wool, and leather, would be prime merchandise. Jacob arrived "penniless," but enriched himself during his stay. Evidence of this is in the Bible record of the gift he sent his brother Esau: 200 female goats, twenty male goats, 200 ewes, twenty rams, thirty milk camels with their colts, forty cows, ten bulls, twenty female donkeys, ten male donkeys (chap. 32:14, 15).

As Abraham continued to move, he came to be known as a Hebrew (chap. 14:13). The origin of this term is unclear, but archeologists are more and more intrigued by a similarly sounding term used in that period and in that general region, "Habiru." This was an epithet referring to a nomad, often used in a derogatory way of a person without roots, and also to denote a "donkey caravaneer."[57] Names given to a people, a church, or an organization often refer to an early practice or custom. These are not always complimentary, but they sometimes stick. As an illustration, one could mention the name Baptist or Anabaptist, a term describing the peculiar emphasis of that group of baptizing by immersion, or Methodists, referring to the methodical religious practices that characterized the founders of that church.

The term "Habiru" had broad significance and did "not apply to any particular nationality, religion or language, but rather to a social or legal status."[58]

In the broadest sense, a Habiru was a foreigner, without a permanent home, and therefore always on the move. This was a rather accurate picture of Abraham. Later, Abraham's descendants, the Israelites, were also known as Hebrews.

Some archeologists point out that when the term "Habiru" came in disuse, so did the term "Hebrew." They see here a definite relationship in the use of the terms.

CHAPTER 8

Aleppo, Ebla, Damascus

And he was called the Friend of God (James 2:23).

How long a time Abraham and his family stayed in Haran we do not know, but after his father, Terah, died at age 205, Abraham, himself 75, followed the call of God and left with his family, his nephew Lot, and his "wealth—the cattle and slaves he had obtained in Haran" (Gen. 12:5, T.L.B.).

The Bible does not mention that Abraham's brother Nahor traveled with Terah and Abraham from Ur, but there is evidence that his descendants lived in Haran (chap. 24:10, 15). Nahor had a son Bethuel, the father of Rebekah and Laban (verses 15, 29), living in Haran. This suggests Nahor himself may have stayed in the city after Abraham left.

The descendants of Nahor became idolatrous in their religion. This practice can be observed through several generations.

Nahor's family was the closest in family ties and in distance to Abraham's descendants in Canaan. This was no doubt the reason why Abraham's son and grandson found themselves wives in Haran.

When Abraham's caravan left Haran, it traveled

through Syria's fertile northland. Even today, the area is fertile, and lush in vegetation. Several important cities dotted the stretch from Haran to Canaan. Carchemish, Aleppo, Ebla, and Damascus were among several on the main route.

Carchemish was only a few days' travel from Haran. Thus a city, which figures prominently on ancient documents of various countries, such as Egypt, Assyria, and Babylon, would be the last city on the Euphrates Abraham would touch. At one time, the Hittites considered Carchemish their capital.

Centuries after Abraham sojourned there, Carchemish was overrun by the armies of several nations. Assyria destroyed it in 717 B.C., and deported its population—an Assyrian custom. Pharaoh-Necho of Egypt, an ally of Assyria, occupied it after Babylonian armies had destroyed Nineveh in 612 B.C. and were pursuing Assyria's armies, which were fleeing toward Haran. Babylon finally defeated the Egyptians at Carchemish in 605 B.C.

Aleppo (Halab) was nearly 150 miles from Haran, on the way to Canaan. A beautiful modern Syrian city with nearly one million inhabitants stands there today. Aleppo's archeological museum houses some of the best ancient artifacts of this area, including a priceless collection from Ebla.

With Damascus and a few other cites, Aleppo claims the distinction of being among the oldest continuously inhabited city. Its name was found in documents at Mari.

Arabs love stories, and they have an ancient

story about Aleppo, or Halab, which means "milk." The legend says that when Abraham came through there, all the people were sick and dying. But when he milked his cows and gave it to the people to drink, they all got well. No wonder Abraham is still their hero, and they call him affectionately *Khalil*—"friend."

It is interesting to note that three times Abraham is called a friend of God by Biblical writers (2 Chron. 20:7; Isa. 41:8; James 2:23), and to this day he is remembered as such by his descendants the Arabs. In fact, if there is one trait of Abraham's Arabs try to emulate, it is friendliness and hospitality. If an Arab invites you to his home or tent and shares his bread with you, you are his friend for life.

From Aleppo, the road Abraham probably followed took a southerly direction, heading toward Canaan. A two- or three-day caravan journey would have taken his party to the outskirts of the royal city of Ebla, the seat of government for some 260,000 people.[59]

Ebla, known today as Tell Mardikh, lay buried and forgotten for many centuries. It was destroyed between the days of Abraham and Moses, and only recently has come back to light again. As I write, it is being excavated by a team of Italian archeologists in cooperation with the Directorate—General of Antiquities and Museum of Syria. In the few years of digging on the site, an enormous amount of evidence and information has been recovered that will greatly enrich our knowledge of the background to the patriarchal age.

One of the more remarkable finds was a royal

archive of some sixteen thousand tablets and fragments of tablets, in beautiful cuneiform script.[60] Much of the writing on them must have been done by expert calligraphists. It is so sharp and beautiful, and so well preserved that it is hard to imagine that these clay tablets may be more than four thousand years old. How good of God to preserve them that we today might see, read, and believe.

An interesting bit of evidence unearthed at Ebla was the name of one of its earlier kings, Ebrum, equivalent to the Biblical name Eber. Abraham had a great-great-great-great-grandfather with that name (Gen. 11:15-27).

According to the chronology of the Bible, Eber lived 464 years, or from 2277 B.C. to 1813 B.C. This suggests that he was contemporaneous with Abraham. If so, the two may have met as Abraham went through his territory.

For Abraham, Ebla may have been a profitable stop, for not only were the people speaking a Semitic dialect that he could probably understand, but, as tablets reveal, the city had active trade contacts with such Canaanite cities as Jerusalem, Sodom, Hazor, Gaza, and others. These were places where Abraham would soon be going, and every bit of information from there must have been valuable to him. In fact, there may have been caravans at Ebla from some of those cities from which the patriarch could gather information. Anciently, it was largely through caravans that news was carried from place to place.

After Ebla, Abraham's travels took him more and more into a new world. Mesopotamia was left behind, and the Mediterranean culture began to unfold. Now the patriarch came in contact with the people of the islands of the sea—the seafaring Phoenicians who dominated commerce, not by caravans, as Abraham was used to, but by ships. Now Abraham saw majestic and coveted cedars, tall and big trees such as were not to be seen in all of Sumeria.

Soon there would also be the Canaanites and Egyptians of whom Abraham may have heard much. These peoples were related to him as far back as Noah's sons, Abraham descending from the son, Shem, and the Canaanites and Egyptians from Ham.

But first, Abraham had to go to Damascus, as no doubt many a caravaneer suggested that he do. It was on the way, in any event.

Although there is no direct mention of Damascus in the Biblical account of Abraham's journey, there is an inference. In Canaan, the patriarch speaks of one of his chief servants, Eliezer of Damascus (chap. 15:2). It is generally conceded that Eliezer joined Abraham's household during the patriarch's stay at the city.[61] In fact, some archeologists, notably W. F. Albright[62] and James Kelso,[63] emphasize that a businessman such as Abraham needed banking connections for his enterprises, but as an alien, loans would not be available to him. So, according to custom, a man approved by the banking establishment, in this case Eliezer, was adopted by Abraham as security. Since the patriarch had no male heirs, Eliezer would inherit and administer Abraham's possessions in case of his death, making sure that all loans were paid to his creditors.

Biblical archeologists suggest that this practice, commonly followed in Mesopotamia, was the reason Abraham and Sarah asked God to accept Eliezer as heir of His promise when they could not have a child of their own. Abraham refers to Eliezer as the steward of his house (verse 2), or the one to be heir of his possessions.

Damascus of Syria was a thriving caravan city in patriarchal times. The Assyrians called it "the City of Asses,"[64] a name probably derived from its practice of breeding black donkeys, known today as Damascus donkeys. These animals lent themselves well for caravan transport because they could carry about twice as much as the ordinary burro.

Damascus is situated in a fertile oasis watered by the Biblical Abana River (modern Barada). Its water, originating from melting mountain snows, was proverbial for its sparkling beauty. Second Kings 5 tells of Naaman, a Syrian army general one thousand years after Abraham, who contracted leprosy and was urged by a Hebrew slave girl of his household to see the prophet Elisha in Israel. The general, whose unexpected presence in Israel nearly caused a war incident, finally got in touch with the prophet. When told by Elisha to wash seven times in the Jordan River, he was outraged, responding angrily, "Are not Abana and Pharpar, rivers of Damascus, better than all the waters of Israel?" (verse 12).

Another interesting incident that confirmed Damascus' place on the Biblical map took place nearly two thousand years after Abraham. This was the conversion of Saul of Tarsus as he approached the city. Saul was going to Damascus to arrest disciples of Jesus who had fled there some time after the death of their Master. But, as the familiar Acts account tells us, Saul was converted, and he too became a disciple. Under the circumstances, he was probably baptized in the Abana River.

Damascus is still a fascinating city, even four thousand years after Abraham's visit there. In some ways, it may not have changed much. The copper workers are still hammering out their wares, and the weavers are still producing beautiful patterns in silk. The other merchants in the *suq* had wares, today even as anciently, from places as far away as China, Egypt, South Arabia, India, Persia, and a host of other ancient countries. How much fun the members of Abraham's caravan must have had here, even as one has today!

CHAPTER 9

Entering the Promised Land

"I will make of you a great nation, and I will bless you, and make your name great" (Gen. 12:2, R.S.V.).

How excited Abraham's caravan must have been when they left Damascus. After traveling for nearly a thousand miles, they were on the last leg of their journey before entering the Promised Land. Because of the prolonged stay at Haran, the whole trip may have lasted a number of years—some suggest as many as twenty-five. My family and I traveled this whole distance from Ur to Canaan to Egypt, using the most varied and sometimes unusual methods of transportation. Other than by air, no matter how one travels over this distance, it is an exhausting experience. And Abraham at age 75 and Sarah at 65 must have felt the same way.

As we do not know the exact routes Abraham took during the first part of his journey, so we do not know the route he took now. As archeologist Roland DeVaux once said, "The routes have left no more imprint in the memory than the passing of the caravans over the sand." [65] However, it really doesn't matter which route was taken, though it would be interesting to know. The important thing is that Abraham and his family made it safely to Canaan.

One thing is sure: if Abraham's trip had taken place today, he would have been stopped at the border of Canaan and either sent back home or made to travel hundreds of miles by way of the Mediterranean. He might even have been forced to go by way of Cypress or Greece, to be granted permission to enter "Israel" legally, except as he might have entered through the Hashemite Kingdom of Jordan and been granted special permission to enter the West Bank via the Allenby Bridge. Knowing Abraham and his way with kings and princes, this is probably what he would have done.

But with the situation as it was in his day, Abraham no doubt crossed into the Promised Land by the Sea of Galilee, the jewel of the country, without any question. On the verdant hillsides and by the clear waters of this lake, six hundred feet below sea level, caravans liked to linger, even as tourists do today. Plenty of fresh fish, lots of fruits, grains, and good water, as well as an abundance of fodder for animals, gave reason for delight as caravans rested here.

Galilee has always been known for its international conglomeration of people. In the time of Jesus, this area was made up largely of a broad-minded Gentile population. But the Biblical account does not mention Abraham as stopping here. His first recorded stop was at the town of Shechem, in the heart of the country. Overnight the population probably doubled with the arrival of Abraham's caravan, for Shechem was not very populous. Of course, the Shechemites were used to this, since it was a town that catered to caravans. Neither may it have caused concern if they learned that this caravan of Sumerians had come to stay in the country. After all, Canaan was made up of representative groups of many nationalities.

Before the times of Israel, the land of Canaan was not a place where a strong country could develop. Even Israel prospered only because of divine providence. It was a territory usually under the control of one or another of the major powers. Most of the time this power was Egypt. At other times it was Babylon or Assyria.

One cannot help wondering what Abraham's first impression of Canaan was and how he felt. Was he disappointed because of its backwardness and lack of culture, as compared with Ur? Was he happy because he had dreams of what the country someday would be, under divine guidance? Was it a challenge to him to have the opportunity to do something creative there? It is hard to imagine, because Abraham rarely recorded any sentiments. He never attempted anything on a large scale along the lines of building a nation, a temple, or a church. He died without owning any more land than the field of his burial ground. Yet he must have been happy to be where God wanted him to be. Maybe this is all God expected of Abraham—just to get out of Ur and go to Canaan, so that God could work, starting in a small way, like a mustard seed implanted in the ground. In time, centuries later, a nation would be raised here—descendants of Abraham—through which God desired to enlighten the world.

In Revelation, John seems to suggest that on occasions, God expects only one major task from an individual, a church, or an organization. He said, "I will put upon you none other burden" (Rev. 2:24). As far as we can determine, Abraham, for the most part, stayed in Canaan and lived an exemplary life. It might be said that nothing of major significance happened. About a century after his death in a foreign country, his descendants left Canaan and moved to Egypt, there to become slaves. For all practical purposes, God's plan in Canaan had ended in failure. But this was not so. God's seeds in the ground sometimes sprout only after many years. Thus it was with God's plan for the land of Canaan.

In fact, while at Shechem, God told Abraham, "Look now toward heaven, and tell the stars, if thou be able to number them: and he said unto him, So shall thy seed be" (Gen. 15:5). What person visiting the Orient has not been amazed at the bright skies at night and impressed by the myriads of stars as if they were the sands on the shores of heaven? Abraham never saw God's promise fulfilled in his day. But he had a promise from God, and that was enough for him. Never was a complaint from him recorded. What faith! No wonder his was made an example, and in the Biblical Hall of Faith (Hebrews 11), Abraham is given more space than any other person.

CHAPTER 10

The Land and the People of Canaan

. . . a land flowing with milk and honey (Ex. 3:8).

A classic description of Canaan in the patriarchal period was circulating in Egypt at the time of Abraham. In it Sinhue, an Egyptian nobleman in political exile, wrote about a visit he made to the area of Canaan and Syria:

> It was a good land, named Yaa. Figs were in it, and grapes. It had more wine than water. Plentiful was its honey, abundant its olives. Every (kind of) fruit was on its trees. Barley was there, and emmer. There was no limit to any (kind of) cattle. . . . Bread was made for me as daily fare, wine as daily provision, cooked meat and roast fowl, beside the wild beasts of the desert.[66]

Several hundred years after Abraham, when Moses spoke of the Promised Land, he referred to it as "a land flowing with milk and honey." This expression is used eight times in the Bible.

To Abraham and his family, who came from a very flat country, the following description might have been very meaningful:

> ". . . a land of hills and valleys, which drinks water by the rain from heaven" (Deut. 11:11, R.S.V.).

Or this:

". . . a land of brooks of water, of fountains and springs, flowing forth in valleys and hills, a land of wheat and barley, of vines and fig trees and pomegranates, a land of olive trees and honey . . . a land whose stones are iron, and out of whose hills you can dig copper" (chap. 8:7-9, R.S.V.).

All this made Canaan sound like paradise, which it seldom, if ever, was. It was God's plan to make Canaan a lush land of rains and springs of water, and much vegetation, but on condition of Israel's obedience. On the other hand, if Israel would not obey, the result would be a wilderness. Let us listen to a section of the antiphonous pronouncements on Mount Gerizim and Mount Ebal, the recital of the blessing and the curses.

"And if you obey the voice of the Lord your God, . . . the Lord your God will set you high above all the nations of the earth. . . . The Lord will open to you his good treasury the heavens, to give the rain of your land in its season. . . . But if you will not obey the voice of the Lord your God, . . . then all these curses shall come upon you and overtake you. . . . The heavens over your head shall be brass, and the earth under you shall be iron. The Lord will make the rain of your land powder and dust" (chap. 28:1-24, R.S.V.).

God had instructed Israel on good soil conservation and even such "modern" concepts as soil rest (Lev. 25:1-7; Ex. 23:11). He even pointed out that if the nation would not follow this instruction He would send them into captivity so the land could rest (Lev. 26:33-35).

It must be understood that Palestine, or Israel, does not have a naturally heavy rainfall. Although the amount varies considerably, most of the land is arid or semi-arid and depends upon artificial irrigation for an abundant plant growth. Only by God's blessing could rain fall sufficiently for prosperous farming.

In the southern area bordering the Negev (desert), where Abraham settled, rainfall is negligible, and prolonged droughts were, and still are, a severe problem. Then, as now, people had to be ingenious water conservationists to survive long, dry seasons.

Although there is no evidence that Canaan's weather or vegetation pattern was ever substantially different from the present, there apparently were times and places where vegetation was more abundant. For instance, the Plain of Sharon, along the Mediterranean coast, has always been fertile to the point of becoming the proverbial Rose of Sharon! The Valley of Jezreel, in the northern sector, was, and still is, the breadbasket of the nation. And the Jordan Valley, once largely irrigated by the overflowing Jordan River, had abundant vegetation. The only areas where vegetation is abundant today is where irrigation is used. All the overflow fresh water is drained from the Sea of Galilee, and even farther north, and channeled to dry and thirsty cities or to some farmlands. Today, the Jordan River is nothing but a trickle of brackish water. Whereas it took a miracle for Israel to be able to cross the Jordan River when Joshua led them, it is no problem to do so today.

In Palestine, archeology has found bones of larger animals, such as elephants, rhinoceroses, and hippopotamuses,[67] animals that required more water and vegetation than is now available. The Bible also mentions such larger animals as the bear, and lions, as well as such creatures hard to identify as the behemoth and the leviathan. These may, in fact, be merely legendary.

Many peoples in patriarchal and post-patriarchal times who inhabited Canaan are listed in several places of the Bible. Moses, who must have been well acquainted with them since he was a prominent figure in Royal Egypt and would know about Canaan, which was under Egyptian control, lists them within the patriarchal context as follows: Kenites, Kenizzites, Kadmonites, Hittites, Perizzites, Rephaim, Amorites, Canaanites, Girgashites, Jebusites (Gen. 15:19-21, R.S.V.). Genesis 10 (verse 15-20) lists descendants of Canaan, grandson of Noah, after whom the land of Canaan was named.

Very little is known of most of these "nations." They may have merged, become absorbed, or died out. A few remained for centuries to come, and are well known Biblically and archeologically. Among these were the Hittites, the Canaanites, the Amorites, and to a lesser degree, the Jebusites.

The Canaanite Hittites were a representative group of the powerful nation by the same name occupying some of the territory known today as Turkey. The main city of the nation, Khattusha, is present-day Boghazkoi. The city has been archeologically excavated by German teams and has produced much information about this powerful, warlike nation of patriarchal times. Nearly a thousand years after Abraham's birth, David had a brave Hittite officer in his army, though the Hittites, as a nation, were extinct at that time.

The Amorites, too, were a powerful, warlike people, some of whom were living in Canaan. Their influence was felt in Egypt and as far away as Ur, Babylon, and Mari. Tablets and papyri mention them.

The Sumerians appear to have developed a particular dislike for these people, whom they called the Amurru. One tablet identifies an Amorite as a savage "who eats raw meat, who has no house in his lifetime, and after he dies, lies unburied."[68] King Ibbi-Sin of Ur spoke of them as vagabonds who had never known what a town was.[69]

The Egyptians, who exercised nominal control over the people of Canaan, seemed to have had their share of trouble with them. Apparently, the Canaanites were not docile and submissive, and the Egyptians did not feel they could rule over them with an iron fist.

Archeologists have uncovered evidence of an interesting way by which the Egyptians got rid of their frustrations over these nations. They call this evidence "Execration Texts." These were usually clay figurines of prisoner soldiers on which names of rulers or cities were written, along with a curse.[70] Since most of these figurines are found broken in pieces, it is believed that they were purposely smashed so that the curse might take effect. Among the figurines is one directed at Shechem.[71] Others were against Jerusalem, Ashkelon, Beth-shean, and many more.

The Amorites and Canaanites were probably the most numerous and influential people in Canaan in patriarchal times. The Canaanites had their subnations named after the sons of Canaan. The term "nations" is to be understood as family groups. Sometimes the term "Canaanite" is used in a geographical sense for all inhabitants of Canaan.

When Israelite spies were sent into Canaan before the conquest, to spy out the country, they reported on the area inhabited by these various people. They said: "The Hittites, and the Jebusites, and the Amorites, dwell in the mountains: and the Canaanites dwell by the sea, and by the coast of the Jordan" (Num. 13:29).

The Bible occasionally speaks of giants living in the land in the days of Moses. The spies reported giants, descendants of Anak (verses 28, 33), compared with which they felt like grasshoppers. Of a slightly later period Og, king of Bashan, is mentioned as being so big that he needed a bedstead about thirteen feet long and six feet wide (Deut. 3:11). Of the days of David, Goliath is mentioned, whose height was nine and one-half feet.

Of the tall people in Canaan in the patriarchal period, the family grouping of the Anakim and the Rephaim are especially mentioned in the Bible. How many of these giants there were is unknown. Possibly not too many, for archeology has never come across bones of giants such as Og or Goliath. Perhaps there were no more giants in Abraham's time than there are in the world today. How many bones of giants would one find in the excavation of the usual cemetery?

Tall men had great advantages when positions of

leadership were to be filled. They were placed in front of armies to give a fearful impression. A king was supposed to be tall. Saul was largely chosen to be Israel's first king because he was well above average in height. So, although possibly small in number, "giants" were more noticeable and made a great impression on people.

Not much was known about the religion of the people of Canaan until the archeological find of Ugarit, modern Ras Shamra, on the Mediterranean coast of Syria. This seaport trading city, which flourished in the patriarchal period, has shed a great deal of light on the culture and religion of Canaan.[72]

They were worshipers of many gods. The main god was called El, his wife was Asherah. Their son was the famous, or infamous, Baal. His wife was Anath, who was the equivalent of the Babylonian Ishtar and known in the Bible as Ashtarte or Ashtoreth. She was the seductive goddess of fertility, love, and war.

Fertility became an obsession among the people of Canaan—fertility of people, flocks, and fields. Fertility cults were promoted in temples, groves, and high places. And in these cults the grossest form of immorality was practiced, the religious and sensual blended.

It was believed that for fertility to exist, the gods must be led into copulative actions and that this would be brought about by their watching orgiastic pleasures among their devotees in religious services on earth.[73]

Sacrificial rites were also common among Canaanite nations. There is Biblical and extra-Biblical evidence for animal and human sacrifices. In some "high places" excavated, such as the Canaanite city of Gezer, human and animal bones were found mixed near altars of sacrifice. Some of these rites were still being practiced when Israel conquered Canaan. So God commanded Israel, "After the doings of the land of Canaan . . . shall ye not do" (Lev. 18:3).

It is no wonder that God decided to make an end to the gross immorality and base religion practiced by the Canaanites. He commanded Israel, "Of the cities of these people . . . thou shalt save alive nothing that breatheth" (Deut. 20:16).

Abraham was not called out of Ur and into Canaan because of a better atmosphere in Canaan. If anything, it was worse. But God had planned for Abraham's descendants to take over the land, and there He wanted them to reveal Him to the world.

CHAPTER 11

Shechem, Bethel, Ai

Abraham and his family finallly arrived in Canaan. Traveling through Canaan, they came to a place near Shechem. . . . Afterwards Abram . . . traveled . . . to the hilly country between Bethel on the west and Ai on the east" (Gen. 12:5-8, T.L.B.).

Long before sunset, the caravaneers customarily sent members of the group ahead to make arrangements for a camping site. No doubt Abraham did what was usually done—permission to camp was sought from the people occupying the land. When approached, the local chief would send his assistant, often a member of his family, to point out an area where the caravan might camp. Whenever possible, this was near a grove where shade and water were available—all for an agreed-upon price, of course.

Whenever possible, Abraham camped near, rather than in, a city. This may have been either by choice or necessity. If his caravan had several hundred people, it would have been difficult to find a caravansary large enough to accommodate all of them, not to mention the animals. So the caravan camped outside of Shechem by the oak at Moreh (verse 6).

Because of its geographical position in Palestine, Shechem is sometimes referred to as "the navel of the country." Its name, meaning "the two shoulders,"[74] was given because the town is situated between two mountains—mountains to become famous in Israelite history centuries later—Mount Ebal and Mount Gerizim.

When Joshua led Israel into the Promised Land, according to a plan outlined by Moses, the nation encamped at Shechem and rehearsed the blessings and the curses God gave them for promise and warning. Six tribes stood on Mount Gerizim and recited the blessings God would bestow upon them if they obeyed and followed Him; the other tribes stood on Mount Ebal and recited the curses that would come if Israel should forsake the Lord and disobey. (Deuteronomy 27, 28). It must have been an impressive occasion for Israel as well as for the onlooking Canaanites.

Abraham's grandson Jacob also encamped at Shechem upon his return from Haran about a hundred years after Abraham's encampment. But unlike Abraham's pleasant experience here, Jacob's sojourn turned into a disaster (Genesis 34). Dinah, Jacob's daughter, who was probably only about 14 years old[75] and an outgoing child, went to Shechem to become acquainted with the girls of the town, but in the process was raped. This, of course, was a great insult to Jacob's family, some of whom planned revenge. When the townsmen sought for reconciliation and friendship, two of Jacob's sons, Simeon and Levi, insisted that the only way for them to establish a friendly relationship would be for their men to be circumcised. This was accepted. When the men were in the greatest pain, Simeon and Levi went into town, massacred the entire male population, rescued Dinah, and plundered the town of its wealth, taking women, children, and animals. Feeling disgraced, Jacob left Shechem. "And Jacob said to Simeon and Levi, Ye have troubled me to make me to stink among the inhabitants of the land" (verse 30).

Before the incident, Jacob had bought the land on which they had camped, and it may have been his purpose to establish himself in the area.

Before Joseph, Jacob's son, died in Egypt, he requested burial in the Land of Promise. His wish was granted, and when the Israelites left Egypt they carried his bones and buried them on Jacob's land in Shechem (Joshua 24:32). The exact location of the tomb is unknown today, but one claimed to be his can be seen in the area.

A more pleasing incident took place near Shechem nearly two thousand years after Abraham's stay there. The area was then known as Samaria. As Jesus came through, He rested at Jacob's well and engaged a Samaritan woman in conversation (John 4). As a result, she and many of the townspeople were converted.

This was about seventeen hundred years after Jacob dug the well, and it was still identified as such in Jesus' day. Even today, near the ruins of old Shechem is a deep well identified as Jacob's well, and there is little reason to doubt its authenticity.[76] Its water is crystal clear, always cool, and never fails. It is located only a few hundred yards from the tomb claimed to be Joseph's.

When we are discussing cities and towns in Canaan, it must be recognized that their size rarely exceeded twenty acres, with a population usually under five thousand. The fact that Simeon and Levi were able to massacre the entire male population of Shechem reveals how small the population must have been.

The old, well-fortified town of Shechem was excavated by German and American teams. Impressive walls and gates are still visible on a site near the modern town of Nablus, though most of the remains are of a period later than Abraham.

From the "city of two shoulders" Abraham moved about thirty miles south to the Canaanite city of Bethel. A spot big enough to accommodate his caravan was found between Bethel and Ai, cities only about two miles apart. This was beautiful terrain, especially in the spring. Even today, there are fruitful valleys, lush grasslands, and hills covered with olive groves. During the spring season this area could indeed be called a land flowing with "milk and honey." Abraham's eyes, and everyone else's in the caravan, must have drunk it all in. "So *this is Canaan!*" they may have said.

Bethel is a Hebrew word for "house of God." Its modern equivalent is Beytin. According to the Biblical account, Bethel was the name given to this place by Jacob about a century after Abraham's stay; the earlier name was Luz (Gen. 28:19). And Abraham encamped on "the mountain on the east of Bethel, and pitched his tent, with Bethel on the west and Ai on the east" (chap. 12:8, R.S.V.). This area, too, was an important caravan center on the main north-south trade road, where it was crossed by the east-west Transjordan route.''[77]

Ai, translated, means "ruins." Archeologists suggest that when Abraham camped here, the city may already have been in ruins.

If there was one thing that must have impressed Abraham about Canaan, it was the enormous quantity of rocks all around. Ur and vicinity had none. Here practically every city had walls and huge fortifications built of rocks, and Ai, as its remains suggest, was no exception.

Both Bethel and Ai have been excavated by various archeological teams, but the results have been meager. While Ai was probably in ruins when Abraham visited there, Bethel was inhabited.[78]

Jerusalem, a rather small and not very significant city, was a mere dozen miles from Bethel. There is no word about Abraham stopping there at this time, but he would do so later, after fighting a bloody battle and delivering his nephew Lot from an invading army. He may also have stopped by a second time while on a mission of sorrow—to offer his son Isaac in sacrifice. Mount Moriah, at that time, was just outside the city of Jerusalem.

Abraham would also return to Bethel after a long sojourn in the south country and Egypt. He would come back here rich and increased in goods. In fact, so many were his head of cattle, sheep, goats, and camels that he and his nephew Lot, who was also rich and who had accompanied him so far, decided to separate.

CHAPTER 12

Egypt

And there was a famine in the land: and Abram went down into Egypt to sojourn there (Gen. 12:10).

It is not known how long Abraham stayed at Bethel. Maybe he was just scouting the country for a good place to settle down. But probably there weren't too many people willing to have another "nation" move in next door. Grazing places were not all that abundant around Bethel, and shepherds were the first to become edgy, as was the case between Abraham's shepherds and Lot's in this very area later on. The account reads: "The land could not support both Abram and Lot with all their flocks and herds. There were too many animals for the available pasture. So fights broke out between the herdsmen of Abram and Lot" (chap. 13:6, 7, T.L.B.).

So Abraham moved to the south country. This area was more sparsely populated—and for a good reason. It was the Negev, the desert. After Abraham arrived there, the country was struck by a severe drought. The patriarch had only two alternatives—move back to the north country and hope to be accepted, or go to Egypt. He chose the latter. A journey of about two hundred miles was involved. For a caravan such as Abraham's, this may have meant a two-week trip over the desert, which brought him to the area of the present Suez Canal. The patriarch had now traveled the whole extent of what is called the Fertile Crescent—a fertile strip of land starting near Ur in Sumer, and extending to the northern portion of Egypt.

Fortunately, Egypt kept good roads open in this area. Its armies often traveled over them to territories it controlled. And caravan traffic from many parts of the Near and Middle East, including Ur, used these routes.[79] This meant that caravansaries were available, food and water certain, and military outposts, for protection and security, added to the peace of mind of the traveler.

Besides, a trip to the magnificent country of the Nile was something every adventurer such as Abraham looked forward to. Egypt and Sumer ranked very close in grandeur and importance, and at the time the former "enjoyed a prosperity seldom matched in all of her long history. . . . It was a golden age of Egyptian culture."[80] Some archeologists also suggest that Abraham needed the business contacts with Egypt to carry on a successful enterprise.

Egypt was generally very hospitable to strangers, especially when they were in need. The regular and usually dependable overflowing of the Nile River would leave a rich loam on many miles of soil. This ensured good harvests every year—enough to feed its own people and those in need.

In Abraham's time, Egypt, like Ur, was developing an extensive water canalization system for irrigation. Some twenty-seven thousand acres of arable land in the Fayyum were added by this means.[81]

Tablets and paintings portray how strangers would often come "skin and bones" to Egypt, and would leave well fed and laden with grain. So it also proved to be in the days of Joseph and his brothers, centuries after Abraham.

Abraham went to Egypt during the powerful Twelfth Dynasty, in many respects the ablest that Egypt ever had.[82] It may be unwise to try to pinpoint it any closer than this, though some suggest that he arrived during the rule of Sen-Usert III (Greek name, Serostris III) from 1887 to 1849 B.C. If this should be correct, then he would be the Pharaoh who appropriated Sarah to himself.

During this period Egypt was engaged in producing bronze, an alloy of copper and tin.[83] For the production of this metal, large mining operations were carried on, one of the main operations being located at Serabit el-Khadim on the Sinai Peninsula.[84] Here mining tunnels, remains of walls, temples, and slag are still visible. These mines were used again centuries later during the rule of the female Pharaoh Hatshepsut. Interestingly, the Sinai is still mined today. When Moses led Israel out of Egypt he promised them, " 'The Lord your God is bringing you into a good land . . . out of whose hills you can dig copper' " (Deut. 8:7-9, R.S.V.).

It is not known where Abraham stayed in Egypt. His caravan probably camped in the northern part by the Delta, where there is much water and pasturage is plentiful. This was the land of Goshen, where his descendants, the Israelites, would live.

Flavius Josephus, a Jewish historian of the first century A.D., makes an interesting comment about Abraham's stay in Egypt. He says that the patriarch "communicated to them arithmetic, and delivered to them the science of astronomy."[85]

Abraham's stay in Egypt may not have been long. His magnaminous spirit, statesmanship, and noble character usually won him respect, admiration, and ready acceptance, but in Egypt he showed that he was still human. He made his first major recorded blunder, which resulted in his expulsion.

Abraham knew of the Egyptians' insatiable admiration for beautiful women, so the patriarch suggested to his wife, Sarah, that she tell everyone that she was his sister.

> "You are very beautiful," he told her, "and when the Egyptians see you they will say, 'This is his wife. Let's kill him and then we can have her!' But if you say you are my sister, then the Egyptians will treat me well because of you, and spare my life" (Gen. 12:11-13, T.L.B.).

When Abraham left Haran he was age 75. The next time his age is given, he was 99 (chap. 17:1). So the patriarch was now between 75 and 99, and Sarah was ten years younger (verse 17). So she was past her "thirty-ninth" birthday. She was perhaps 70, and still coveted for her beauty! Apocryphal literature has much to say about Sarah's exceptional beauty. After living "out of a suitcase" for years, and traveling over dusty roads and under a baking sun for more than a thousand miles, this fact is amazing.

As was foreseen, word got around, and "everyone spoke of her beauty" (verse 14, T.L.B.). And, as

Abraham had predicted, Sarah ended up in Pharaoh's harem.

Abraham's suggestion that Sarah say he was her brother was not a lie; she was his half-sister (chaps. 11:29; 20:12). But neither was it the whole truth. The patriarch's motive in telling a partial truth was to save his life—regardless of what this meant for his wife.

One should not look at this close family intermarriage totally from the cultural point of view of our twentieth century, or the picture will be distorted. Such marriages were, and still are, common in the Middle East. In spite of the congenital effects it was encouraged to preserve the family wealth and possessions and to keep the family, tribe, or dynasty intact. Marriages outside of the larger family were discouraged by charging a greater dowry of a groom from a distant place.

Another point to remember is that for any woman to be chosen a member of a king's harem was a great honor. A case in point is Esther when she competed to become a member of Ahasuerus' harem (Esther 2). But marital ties were usually respected—even by kings (Gen. 12:18-20).

Abraham fared well with "his sister" in the king's harem, and was the recipient of royal gifts (verse 16). But the truth was discovered, "and Pharaoh sent them out of the country under armed escort—Abraham, his wife, and all his household and possessions" (verse 20, T.L.B.).

Abraham became *persona non grata* in Egypt and, as far as we know, never returned there.

CHAPTER 13

The South Country

Abram was very rich in cattle, in silver, and in gold (Gen. 13:2).

Abraham's aborted stay in Egypt may have been very brief. The drought in the south of Canaan, which forced him to go to Egypt, may not even have been over yet, which may have been the reason for his return to Bethel, in central Canaan, on this occasion.

At this point, Abraham and his nephew Lot were so wealthy and their cattle so numerous that that many grazing animals could not be supported in one region, in addition to the cattle of the local population, so they decided to part. In his usual generous spirit, Abraham offered Lot the choice of direction in which to go, and Lot chose the lush region of the Jordan Valley, while Abraham took the south, the Negev, or desert. We cannot know how the patriarch felt in his heart about Lot's selfish choice and about his permanent departure, for the two had been together for a long time and had shared many experiences.

With the departure of Lot and his family, cattle, and wealth, Abraham's house may have looked empty, like a home when the children move out.

And the Lord comforted him, " 'I am going to give you so many descendants that, like dust, they can't be counted!' . . . Then Abram moved his tent to the oaks of Mamre, near Hebron" (verses 16-18, T.L.B.).

It is only about twenty-five miles from Bethel to Hebron. Once again, as was the patriarch's custom, he put up his tents outside the city, by the oaks of Mamre. The area between Hebron and Beersheba became Abraham's home for the rest of his life. Long-distance wandering had finally come to an end for him.

Hebron was a name given to the town after the days of Abraham, as was also the case with Bethel, Dan, and others. It must be understood that the patriarch did not write this account; Moses wrote it hundreds of years later, using names by which the towns were known in his days. Hebron's earlier name was Kirjatharba (Joshua 14:15). Its present Arab name is el-Khalil ("the friend"; i.e., Abraham). It had the reputation of being a city of much-feared tall people, the descendants of Anakim (Num. 13:28-32). Nearly a thousand years after Abraham, David made Hebron his first capital before taking Jerusalem from the Jebusites.

The area of Mamre-Hebron being on the point where roads converged from east and west, and north and south,[86] was very advantageous to Abraham. It was the business center in West Palestine that handled all the trade from across Jordan, and from such cities as Sodom and Gomorrah. It is possible that Abraham and Lot maintained lucrative business ties.[87] Also, Hebron was a great caravan center, places which Abraham seemed to favor. Even in Islamic times, centuries after Christ, the city was still a caravan center.[88]

As Abraham pursued his peaceful trade, a new experience awaited him. Rumblings of war were heard from the part of the world with which he was most familiar—Mesopotamia. The record in Genesis 14 has a familiar ring for the cause of ancient wars. A number of cities in the Transjordan, specifically the area east of the Dead Sea, among which were Sodom and Gomorrah, had been conquered at one point and made tributaries to some eastern nations. For twelve years they paid tribute, then stopped. This was always cause for the conquering nations to return and reconquer. In the process much booty was carried away. Lot and his family were also taken captive, along with the other inhabitants. According to practice, they would have become slaves.

As news reached Abraham through an escapee, he mobilized his personal army of 318 men and led them in pursuit of the invaders. He found them camped at Dan, the northernmost city of Israel. Dividing his men in groups, a tactic also used by Gideon, Abraham pounced upon the unexpectant enemy at night, causing panic among them and smiting and pursuing them as they fled, even as far as Damascus.

There are some interesting points to be observed here. The Biblical account mentions that Abraham had treaties with allies (Gen. 14:13), which were probably self-defense treaties in case of an enemy attack. Abraham was a wise and able diplomat. In many instances, we find actions involving treaties, covenants, agreements. He was familiar with local laws and customs, and used them for protection and advantage.

In the case of the 318 "trained men" (verse 14, R.S.V.), they were fighters used for the protection of caravans when they were attacked by marauding bands. Abraham himself led his commandos. We can now add to the qualities of Abraham that of a brave and skillful soldier who knew how to lead an army against what must have been a vastly outnumbering enemy.

Caravans often carried extremely valuable loads such as gold, silver, silk, spices, incense, and other rich commodities. Thievery and attacks on caravans were, consequently, common occurrences in the Middle East, as tablets inform us.[89]

Caravan routes often had military outposts manned by the nation or city through which they passed. Some nations even offered military escorts. Of course, all of this cost money, and to compensate for it, taxes or tolls were collected, which sharply increased the cost of the merchandise carried by caravans.

After Abraham rescued Lot and his family, as well as many others also taken captive, and retrieved the booty, he returned by way of Jerusalem, or Salem,[90] as the record states (verse 18). At this time he gave a tithe to Melchizedek, king of Salem. It is interesting that this is the first mention of Jerusalem, a small Jebusite city. Perhaps Abraham purposely sought out Melchizedek here, a godly king and priest of Jehovah (Ps. 110:4), to whom he could entrust what may possibly have been a sizable tithe.

Tithing was not a new custom, neither was it peculiar to the faith of the patriarchs; it was practiced in the temples of Ur, where the gods claimed to own everything and where the people were considered tenants of the gods.[91]

Following these experiences, Abraham returned to his oaks of Mamre home near Hebron. At this point he was in his 80s and still childless, in spite of God's promise to make a great nation of his descendants. It was here that Sarah decided to follow an old Mesopotamian custom of giving her husband a slave woman so that through her he might have a child. The slave was Hagar, who was probably a gift of Pharaoh in that ill-fated experience in Egypt.

A son was born, and they called him Ishmael, that is, "God hears" (Gen. 16:11, margin, R.S.V.). Even though God promised Ishmael a great blessing, he was not to be the heir.

It was at the oaks of Mamre that God changed the name of the patriarch and his wife, from Abram to Abraham, and from Sarai to Sarah (chap. 17:5, 15). These new names were to remind them of God's covenant with them.

Another sad occurrence marred the patriarch's life while at Mamre: God revealed to him His decison to destroy Sodom and Gomorrah. This will be dealt with in a later chapter.

Once again Abraham struck tent and moved. The reason for his doing this is unknown. This time the destination is farther into the desert—first Gerar, in the southwestern corner of Canaan, and then Beersheba (chaps. 20:1; 21:31), the southernmost city in the kingdom of Israel. Hence the expression "from Dan even to Beersheba" (Judges 20:1). This place is on the northern fringes of the Sinai Peninsula, and is a semimarginal area with a yearly rainfall of from four to eight inches.[92] Here water is worth its weight in gold and one thanks God for every drop. David, in Psalm 63:1, described the area as "a dry and weary land where no water is" (R.S.V.).

One wonders how people could live here; yet when the Israeli archeologist Nelson Glueck combed this area for signs of ancient occupation, he found it had been dotted with villages in the days of Abraham.

The Negev has an attraction all its own, as desert dwellers will recognize. Nature somehow has a way of compensating itself. Although denuded of vegetation, the mountains are majestic, especially when seen in silhouette against the deep-blue sky. There is an occasional oasis where tamarisk trees grow and flowers bloom, even in late summer.

After the winter rains, the Negev turns on its magic. The seeds lying dormant are just waiting to be awakened by the showers, and overnight, as it were, the desert puts on a show unequaled anywhere—lush grass, unending carpets of flowers, birds filling the air, and animals growing fat.

Although not abundant, water is available in the Negev. In Abraham's days, as with the Bedouins living in the area today, people had to learn to live with a small amount of water. Dwellers in the Negev also learned to locate underground pools and streams and to tap them, as well as learning the best ways to catch the precious drops that heaven would send and to save them to be used as needed. They found ways to store water in cisterns and even in porous ground. They also built dams to hold water and to force it into the ground for agricultural purposes. As centuries passed, the desert dwellers improved their techniques to include the building of aqueducts, channels, diversionary wells, and reservoirs, the using of the side of whole mountains as catchment basins, and the employing of extensive water-spreading devices.[93]

It is amazing what water will do for the desert. Nowhere is this better seen than in the very area where Abraham lived, near Beersheba. Today, the modern Israeli nation is accomplishing wonders in this area. Lush fields of fruit, wheat, cotton, and many other agricultural products grow in profusion in places once thought totally unproductive.

It was here, at age 100 for Abraham and 90 for Sarah, that God's promise of a son was fulfilled. They called him Isaac ("laughter"). In these rugged surroundings, the son grew up. It was also here that Hagar and Ishmael were dismissed from the household and left to wander aimlessly in the desert, where Ishmael nearly died of thirst. But God spared his life and eventually made a great nation of him.

As Isaac grew, he must have been the joy of his parents. However, for a short time—time whose hours may have felt like an eternity—this joy was to be broken. The account of God's call for Abraham to sacrifice his son is one of the most dramatic stories in the Bible.

And God said to Abraham, " 'Take your son,

your only son Isaac, whom you love, and go to the land of Moriah, and offer him there as a burnt offering' " (Gen. 22:2, R.S.V.).

Genesis 22 contains what E. A. Speiser terms "the profoundest personal experience in all recorded history of the patriarchs; and the telling of it soars to comparable literary heights." [94]

The command must have stunned the patriarch. Yet the account suggests that he remained rational and trusted God, believing that God could raise his son even from the dead (Heb. 11:19).

Even from Ur, Abraham was familiar with the custom of offering human sacrifice. The sacrifice of human victims as substitutes for kings and queens was practiced. As has been mentioned, in one tomb, Woolley's "death-pit," seventy-four victims were found. This was just one of sixteen tombs found with varying numbers of human sacrifices.[95]

Even in the New World, in Mexico and Guatemala, perhaps as early as a thousand years before Christ, the chests of captive soldiers were cut open and the still-pulsating heart removed as an offering.[96] In Canaan, too, human sacrifice was practiced,[97] the Biblical account on this is clear (Judges 11:30, 31; 1 Kings 16:34).

One wonders whether Abraham's knowledge of these practices weighed on his mind.

The journey from his home in the southland to the appointed place, Mount Moriah, took Abraham three days (Gen. 22:4). Although archeologists are not unanimous in locating Mount Morah, many accept the traditional site, that is, the hill that in those days was just outside the Jebusite city of Jerusalem.

It wasn't until the days of David and Solomon, nearly a thousand years after Abraham, that the hill was annexed to the city and the Temple built there. With the destruction of the Temple by the Romans in 70 A.D., the area remained without any major structure until the Moslems built the Dome of the Rock by which they honor both Abraham's sacrifice and Mohammed's flight to heaven. In spite of the problems between Ishmael and Isaac, Arabs seem to have forgiven Abraham for his actions toward Ishmael, their progenitor.

But Isaac was not sacrificed, though the faith of Abraham and Isaac was tested to the limit.

"The angel of the Lord called to him from heaven, and said, 'Abraham, Abraham!' And he said, 'Here am I.' He said, 'Do not lay your hand on the lad or do anything to him; for now I know that you fear God, seeing you have not withheld your son, your only son, from me' " (verses 11, 12, R.S.V.).

Abraham had met the supreme test, and his faith in God was complete, even to the point of not withholding his own son. In the eyes of the universe, God was justified in making Abraham the father of the faithful. He trusted God fully.

A few years passed. Abraham and his family were living at Hebron (chap. 23:2). Then Sarah died at the age of 127 (verse 1). Isaac was 37 years old at that time, and Abraham had reached the vintage age of 137. To that moment, Abraham owned not an inch of land. The death of his wife forced him to choose either to bury her in a single grave or to purchase a cave where a whole family could be put to rest. He chose the latter.

It is interesting to observe in the Biblical record the procedure in the purchase of a burial ground (chapter 23). Even today, in certain areas of the Middle East, the purchase of anything, from a loaf of bread to a piece of land, calls for ceremony and a diplomacy that apparently even four milleniums have not changed.

Abraham, as a foreigner (verse 4), must first address the people of that land to win their approval, making it possible for him to purchase land. Their willingness secured, he bowed respectfully in gratitude.

He next communed with them (verse 8). A buyer should not be in too great a hurry to consummate a purchase, even today. There must be time to talk about the family, to eat a meal or at least sip some tea, and then back to the deal.

Abraham then solicited the community to intercede with the owner to sell him the land. Actually he may have been even eager to sell. This accomplished, Abraham specified the exact piece of land he wished. All of this was done in the presence of many onlookers.

For the consummation of the deal, both parties had to go to the city gate, where all such transactions were executed in the sight of witnesses (verse 10).

"But how much is the price?" "Oh, nothing," the owner might reply. Such conversation was not to be taken seriously, of course; it was only a matter of being polite (verse 11). "Take it, take it," he might even urge. This gesture must be met with another polite gesture, and Abraham bowed and accepted it, realizing that the generous offer must be met with another generous offer of payment.

The price was finally revealed—400 shekels of silver. Usually, haggling for the right price would then begin. But under the circumstances, Abraham was not eager to follow the normal procedure, so he paid the inflated, exorbitant price by weighing out the required amount. Abraham recognized that he was at a disadvantage and that the landowner could ask for almost any price and get it. Not only was the buyer a foreigner; he was also rich, and he needed the land on that very day so that his loved one could be buried.

That the price was excessive is clearly shown when we read that Omri paid 6,000 shekels for the entire site of Samaria (1 Kings 16:24), and Jeremiah gave only seventeen shekels for land probably as large as the field of Machpelah (Jer. 32:9). In fact, in patriarchal days whole villages were sold for from one hundred to one thousand shekels, as tablets from Syria indicate.[98]

Anciently, caves were commonly used as burial places in Canaan. The land had many of these and they became natural places for graves. Archeologists have uncovered many such cemeteries, and the evidence suggests that after a person had been buried for a while and another person died, the bones of the former would simply be pushed aside to make room for the new body. Thus many people could be buried in one cave. Some think that this gives significance to the Biblical expression concerning one who died, saying that he was "gathered to his people" (Gen. 25:8; 35:29).

Sarah was buried in the cave Abraham bought, the cave of Machpelah (chap. 23:19). Later, Abraham (chap. 25:10), Isaac (chap. 35:29), Rebekah (chap. 49:31), Leah (chap. 49:31), and Jacob (chap. 50:13) were interred there also.

Burial places are an excellent source of information for archeologists. Not only do they inform us of burial customs, but they often contain pottery, objects of adornment, and other articles of personal use. The bones also give information, such as the gender and approximate size of the deceased. Sometimes they reveal the cause of death, and diseases of the body affecting the bones.

With the purchase of the field from the people of Heth, Abraham, the nomad, had become a landowner.[99]

Three years after the death of his mother, Isaac, now age 40 (chaps 23:1; 25:20), and still single, decided to get married. Concerned that his son might marry a Canaanite, Abraham suggested that a wife be found for him from among their relatives left behind in Haran. According to custom, this important choice was not left to the son. Such matters were decided either by the father or by one whose judgment the father could fully trust. Eliezer of Damascus, Abraham's most dependable servant and steward of the household, was selected for the task.

A small caravan was readied for the nearly one-thousand-mile round trip, and was laden with both provisions for the trip and priceless objects of silver and gold and pieces of silk, probably from Damascus (chap. 24:53).

The gifts were to be part of the dowry, which in this case had to be large, because the groom was not only unknown but from another country. This increased the risks for the bride and her family. The dowry would become the possession of the bride, to be used by her in case of divorce.

Eliezer's trip was successful beyond expectation. The woman he met at the well, Rebekah, the daughter of Bethuel, who was the son of Nahor (verse 15), was the one he decided should be Isaac's wife. Nahor was Abraham's brother who had stayed at Haran (chap. 22:23). Isaac, therefore, married the daughter of a cousin, But, as we pointed out previously, this is not an uncommon practice in the Middle East, even today.

The decision was quickly made, and all felt the leading of God in the matter. Rebekah went with Eliezer and became Isaac's wife, and "he loved her" (chap. 24:67).

CHAPTER 14

Sodom and Gomorrah

Lot dwelt among the cities of the valley and moved his tent as far as Sodom (Gen. 13:12, R.S.V.).

When Abraham was still living in the plains of Mamre, near Hebron, God sent some emissaries to him with a message of doom to the cities of the valley, east of the Dead Sea. Among these were Sodom and Gomorrah (chapter 18).[100] This was the verdant and prosperous valley that Lot had selected as his homestead.

This valley is part of the great Jordan Rift, earth's deepest canyon. Nelson Glueck has suggested that if a man on the moon looked toward the earth, it would be one of the few peculiar features discernible.[101]

The Rift starts south of the Hermon and Lebanon mountains on the Syrian border. Like a deepening trough, it runs southward, forming the depression filled by the water of the Sea of Galilee, whose surface is 685 feet below sea level. The Rift gradually declines in its southerly path, forming the Jordan River and reaching its lowest point in the bed of the Dead Sea at approximately 2,500 feet below sea level, though the surface of the Dead Sea is now about 1,300 feet below sea level. This makes the Dead Sea, which is about forty-eight miles long and eleven miles wide, the lowest lake on earth. The Rift continues through the Red Sea and into the African continent.

The Dead Sea has another distinction, in that it is the saltiest large body of water on the globe, having about 28 percent sodium chloride (ordinary salt) as compared to about 5 percent for ocean water. For this reason it is sometimes called the Salt Sea. Diving here is practically impossible; the human body floats like a cork. The density of the brime is so strong that life in it in any form is impossible. This salt concentration is the result of water continually entering the Dead Sea and not being able to escape except through evaporation. This process of distillation, as it were, leaves not only sodium chloride but potassium, natron, chlorine, and compounds of manganese, calcium, and bromide.[102]

There is no evidence that this condition was ever different in ancient times. The lake was, therefore, useless except for salt, which, of course, was a useful commodity, though quite abundant. The extraction of potash from rich fields of minerals has made the area economically desirable. Companies from various parts of the world operate around the clock here.

The Dead Sea is undergoing unusual changes today. Whereas until recently its level was slowly but steadily rising because more water entered than evaporated, today it is steadily dropping. The heavy usage of fresh water for farming, and supply of cities, has placed a heavy demand upon the water of the

Sea of Galilee and even farther north. This has resulted in a great reduction in the flow of the Jordan River. So serious is this problem that the State of Israel is planning to pump water from the Mediterranean, over the mountains, into the Dead Sea. Because of the great difference in sea level, a waterfall effect will be produced that will generate electricity, as well as replenish the Dead Sea. Evaporation will continue, along with the formation of salt and other minerals. Today the extraction of minerals from the Dead Sea is a major economic benefit for both countries bordering it, Israel and Jordan.

Because of the abundance of water flowing down the Jordan River in patriarchal times, with beneficial periodic floodings, the area was lush with vegetation. This in turn generated moisture and rain benefiting an even wider area. The Biblical account explains that the plain of Jordan "was well watered everywhere, before the Lord destroyed Sodom and Gomorrah, even as the garden of the Lord." (chap. 13:10).

Archeologists have looked for the cities of the plain for more than a hundred years; historians and interested travelers have done so even longer. Until recently, most scholars were suggesting that since the level of the Dead Sea had been rising continually over the centuries, the cities were probably under the water. Others suggested that the Biblical account on this point was not to be taken seriously.

Three things are changing previous views. One, because the Dead Sea is drying up, more and more areas once covered by water are visible. But it has become clear that there are no ruins there.

Two recent archeological evidence uncovered at Ebla, a city of patriarchal times, hints strongly at commercial ties between that city and cities east of the Jordan and the Dead Sea.[103] The director of the Ebla excavation, Paolo Matthiae, mentions that the name "Saduma" appears, but suggests that this may not refer to Sodom at all.[104] Although no sure deductions can be drawn from this statement, and publication of the tablets must be awaited, at least the possibility is there that extra-Biblical information may soon be available about the cities of the plain.

The third point of evidence is perhaps the most exciting. In 1965, archeologist Paul Lapp started excavating some remains of ancient sites east of the Dead Sea. In 1975, archeologists Walter Rast and Thomas Schaub resumed the excavations and have confirmed the existence of the remains of five cities east of the Dead Sea. Their present names are, from north to south: Bab edh-Dhra, Numeira, Safi, Feifa, and Khanazir.[105] The Biblical names were: Sodom, Gomorrah, Admah, Zeboim, and Bela, which is also called Zoar (chap. 14:2). Some archeologists are cautiously optimistic that these may be the same.

These ruins are basically situated in the area where it was earlier thought the cities might be, that is, southeast of the Dead Sea—except that they are above the water level instead of below. The ruins, separated from each other by a few miles, are on a low plateau of about two hundred feet elevation above the Dead Sea level that formed the valley, and about a mile from where the water once reached.

The area is now practically denuded of all except some low vegetation that serves as food for goats.

In spite of desertlike conditions, and intense heat and humidity in the summer, some people still live here by Bahr Lut, "Sea of Lot," as the Arabs call it. These people are mostly Bedouins, and Negroes from the Sudan whose ancestors were brought here as slaves during the days of the Ottoman Empire.

Rainfall is about two inches per year; some springs of fresh water make life possible.

The side east of the Dead Sea is part of the Hashemite Kingdom of Jordan.

As a background for the ancient cities, the Jordanian mountains, or the mountains of Moab, as they were anciently called, rise sharply from an altitude of three hundred feet below sea level to five thousand feet above. These are the mountains to which people fled when eastern armies invaded the cities of the valley (verse 10) and to which Lot was urged to flee when told to leave Sodom (chap. 19:17).

The Bible mentions the existence of slime pits, perhaps better known today as tar or asphalt wells, near the cities (chap. 14:10). Tar was still found in the lake in the early centuries before Christ, and because of it, Greek writers referred to it as Lake Asphaltitis. This asphalt was often shipped to Egypt, where it was used for medicinal purposes and for embalming.[106]

The Bible speaks of the cities of the plain not only as beautiful "as the garden of the Lord" (chap. 13:10), but prosperous, which brought the unfortunate consequences "pride, fulness of bread, and abundance of idleness" (Eze. 16:49).

This life of plenty and ease had its effect upon the inhabitants of Sodom and Gomorrah. Their sinful condition became proverbial, prophet after Hebrew prophet referring to it. Isaiah points out the lack of justice (chaps. 1:10; 3:9); Jeremiah mentions their moral depravity (Jer. 23:14); Ezekiel speaks of their disregard to the poor (chap. 16:49). The divine messengers to Abraham emphasized that their sin was "very great" (Gen. 18:20).

Canaanite religion was, as we have seen, at great variance to a life of purity. The Canaanites not only condoned but fostered acts of immorality, feeling that in so doing, the gods themselves would imitate them, and thus fertility in people, cattle, and fields would be assured.

As the angel emissaries from God entered Sodom, they were met by Lot, who was at the city gate when they arrived. This may be an indication that Lot had achieved a certain distinction with the citizens and occupied a position of leadership. The gate was more than an entrance to a city; it was the focal point of city life. Perhaps it was like a city hall where civil business was transacted.

Lot immediately invited the strangers to become his guests at his house. Being well aware of the immorality of the citizens, he was eager to protect the visitors. But word was getting around. Wherever a stranger enters a village in the Middle East, even today, he is quickly observed.

Soon the men of the city went to Lot's house and demanded to have homosexual relations with Lot's guests. To God, this was probably the last straw.

After getting Lot and his family from the city, "the Lord rained upon Sodom and Gomorrah brimstone and fire from the Lord out of heaven" (chap. 19:24).

Scholars have tried to suggest natural ways for the destruction of the cities. A volcanic destruction, the most apparent from the description, must be ruled out because no volcanic evidence is available.

Some suggest that an earthquake released underground gases, which ignited. The area is earthquake-prone, and asphalt pits are spoken of in the Biblical account. If God used such methods as the account suggests, it cannot be proved. In any case, the cities were completely destroyed, whether by natural or unnatural means. The ruins being excavated today in the area suggest that they were destroyed or abandoned and never again inhabited.

> And Abraham got up early in the morning to the place where he stood before the Lord: and he looked toward Sodom and Gomorrah, and toward all the land of the plain, and beheld, and, lo, the smoke of the country went up as the smoke of a furnace (verses 27, 28).

Lot escaped with his two daughers, and they fled to the little town of Zoar. In the actions that followed, the family gave evidence that the spirit of Sodom was also theirs. Desiring offspring, the daughters got their father drunk and had intercourse with him, and eventually each had a child. The son of the elder daughter was named Moab; the younger named her son Ammon. These became the heads of two nations, the Moabites and the Ammonites, which established themselves in the territory east of the Dead Sea.

CHAPTER 15

The Father of Nations

"To your descendants will I give this land" (Gen. 12:7, R.S.V.).

"I will multiply your descendants as the stars of heaven and as the sand which is on the seashore" (chap. 22:17, R.S.V.).

Abraham never lived to see the land of Canaan populated with his descendants, but he made a good start in that direction. It might even have been fulfilled sooner than it was had all his children stayed in Canaan. As it was, only the descendants of Isaac—actually, only those from Isaac's son Jacob, stayed in Canaan. All the others went either south or east.

Before Abraham died at age 175 (chap. 25:7), he had eight sons. The first was Ishmael by Hagar, the second was Isaac by Sarah and after Sarah's death, he had six more by Keturah (verses 1, 2). Both Hagar and Keturah were called concubines (verse 6).

Ishmael married an Egyptian woman and dwelt in the wilderness of Paran (chap. 21:21), which is the Negev of the Sinai Peninsula. He had twelve sons, who became princes of tribal families. His descendants kept their father's name and called themselves Ishmaelites. Ishmaelites, then, are part Hamitic through Hagar, and part Semitic through Abraham. They led nomadic lives, mostly in the Arabian Desert and Syria. God's blessing to them was that they would become a great nation, which has indeed been fulfilled. Among their famous descendants were the Nabateans, who centuries later established themselves in the land of the Edomites, south of the Dead Sea. They were expert craftsmen, carving exquisite buildings into the rocks of the old city of Petra. They became skillful in hydraulics and built dams and other intricate water-conservation measures in the desert. Arabs trace their ancestry to Ishmael.

One of Ishmael's daughters, Mahalath, married Isaac's son Esau (chap. 28:9). Thus the Ishmaelites and Edmonites, as the descendants of Esau were known, became related.

Six sons were born to Keturah. Abraham gave them gifts and sent them eastward (chap. 25:6). The one to become best known through his descendants was Midian. The Midianites settled in the area around the eastern branch of the Red Sea, called the Gulf of Aqabah. Southern Sinai may have been part of their territory, where Jethro, Moses' father-in-law, was priest. So, through Moses, a descendant of Isaac, and Jethro, a descendant of Midian and Keturah, the Midianites and Levites were reunited (Ex. 3:1; 2:21).

The Ishmaelites and Midianites may have stayed close together and cooperated in their labors. As always, making a living from desert lands was difficult so they became caravaneers. The caravaneers who purchased Joseph and sold him in Egypt are described as being Ishmaelites and Midianites (Gen. 37:25, 36). The history of the Ishmaelites and Midianites continued for centuries after Abraham.

A group of people apparently closely associated with the Midianites were the Kenites. In fact, at times the names of the two groups seem to be used interchangeably. The family into which Moses married sometimes is spoken of as Midianite and sometimes as Kenite (Judges 1:16; Num. 10:29).

If the Kenites were a tribe, their origin is unknown. Some suggest they are linked to Kenath (Num. 32:42), a Canaanite town, or Kenaz, a grandson of Esau (Gen. 36:9, 11). Others suggest that the term "Kenite" should not be interpreted as a proper noun but as a profession. A *qeni* was a "smith," and the Kenites were a people who became experts in metal extraction and manufacture.

The Sinai is rich in copper and iron and was worked by the Egyptians. The Kenites are first mentioned in connection with Sinai. Moses was anxious for their aid in traveling through this wilderness, so he invited Hobab, his Kenite brother-in-law (Judges 1:16), to join him.

> And Moses said to Hobab the son of Reuel the Midianite, Moses' father-in-law, "We are setting out for the place of which the Lord said, 'I will give it to you'; come with us, and we will do you good; for the Lord has promised good to Israel." But he said to him, "I will not go; I will depart to my own land and to my kindred." And he said, "Do not leave us, I pray you, for you know how we are to encamp in the wilderness, and you will serve as

eyes for us" (Num. 10:29-31, R.S.V.).

Hobab agreed and traveled with Israel. From that time on, members of his family lived with the Israelites and settled in the Promised Land with them.

Isaac was to be the main line of Abraham's descendants—" 'through Isaac shall your descendants be named,' " God promised Abraham (Gen. 21:12, R.S.V.). So Abraham "gave all he had" to Isaac (chap. 25:5), although he probably gave substantial gifts to all his sons (verse 6).

To Isaac and Rebekah were born twins, Esau and Jacob (verses 24-26). Esau did not care to marry within the family. He chose for himself two Hittite women (chap. 26:34) and, perhaps to appease his parents, he also married a daughter of Ishmael (chap. 36:3).

Esau, as we have seen, became the father of the Edomites, who for the most part inhabited land south of the Dead Sea. Two important Edomite cities are mentioned. One was Teman, named after a grandson of Esau (Gen. 36:11); it has only tentatively been located. It became known for its men of wisdom (Jer. 49:7). One of Job's comforters came from there (Job 2:11).

The other city, which was the Edomite capital, was Sela, meaning "rock," better known today by its Greek equivalent, Petra, also meaning "rock." The Edomites built their city in a place surrounded by a natural wall of mountains. It has an entrance about ten feet wide, formed by a split in the mountain, which the Arabs call a *siq*. It is about a mile long. The walls of mountains and the unusual entryway rendered Petra almost unconquerable. The city was near the king's highway, and the Edomites profited handsomely from caravan traffic.

The Edomites became a powerful and much-feared nation. When Israel left Egypt under Moses, they asked their ancestor-brethren for passage over the king's highway, but were denied (Num. 20:14ff).

The Amalekites split off from the Edomites. Amalek was Esau's grandson (Gen. 36:12, 16). The Amalekites lived west of the Edomites, or south of Canaan. They too were a warlike nation. A good exhibit of this was their attack from the rear upon Israel after the Israelites escaped from Egyptian captivity.

From all these nations, or at least several of them, have come the various Arab tribes. Their hatred toward the descendants of Jacob had become proverbial, and is still in existence today.

The remaining group of people descended from Abraham, the father of nations, are Isaac's descendants through his son Jacob—the Jews. This is the people who conquered the land of Canaan.

CHAPTER 16

Patriarchal Customs

"There is today no reason to doubt the authenticity of the general background of the patriarchal narratives. . . . Lives like theirs [the patriarchs], full of apparent insignificant incidents, can now be duplicated or reconstructed, almost incident by incident, from a number of cuneiform records."—E. A. Speiser, Annual of the American Schools of Oriental Research, *vol. 13, p. 43.*

Among the more fascinating contributions archeology has made confirming the patriarchal age are the records of customs and legal transactions of four thousand years ago. As these are compared to the Biblical record and found to match, they become links verifying the Biblical account.

We sometimes wonder why the Bible includes certain details that to some are boring to read and would seem to have no significance to one's salvation. An example is the detailed account of the transactions accompanying the purchase of the cave of Machpelah, or all the "begats" in Genesis 10 and 11, and other seemingly unending genealogies. But to the archeologist, and the historian, as well as to many other serious students of the Bible, these are often bits and pieces of great significance, not so much in that they are involved with one's salvation but that they confirm the historicity and accuracy of the Biblical record. Every detail in the Bible, one could say, is of significance to somebody.

When Abraham was unable to have children through his wife, Sarah, and they tried until she was about age 75, Sarah offered the Egyptian slave Hagar to Abraham (Gen. 16:1-4), that through her they might have a child. We know now that this was the accepted form, not according to God, but according to Mesopotamian tradition. The following contract recorded on a tablet illustrates the custom in patriarchal times. The original names are changed to Abraham and Sarah to help the reader more easily see the connection.

> If . . . [Sarah] bears [children] . . . Abraham shall not take another wife; but if . . . [Sarah] does not bear . . . [Sarah] shall acquire a woman of the land of Lullu as wife for . . . [Abraham], and . . . [Sarah] may not send her offspring away.[107]

Several points are of interest here, as this account is compared to Abraham's experience.

First, taking a concubine when a wife was unable to bear children was an accepted custom. Second, in such a case it was, wisely, the wife's prerogative to find a substitute to herself to be given to her husband, not the husband's choice. The woman selected was from the land of Lullu, that is, a country from where slaves were obtained. She would be a slave, as Hagar was. Third, the offspring could not be sent away. This helps us understand Abraham's great reluctance to send Ishmael away when Sarah insisted that he do so. It was not merely because of his love for the child, but also because it was against the law. It was not until the Lord instructed him to do so that he finally did agree (chap. 21:9-14).

Jacob's gaining the birthright from Esau also has precedents in history. Although he and his brother, Esau, were twins, Esau was born first and therefore was to be the recipient of the primogeniture, or the birthright, a normally prized privilege. Foremost among the duties of the firstborn was to be the spiritual leader, which responsibilities did not usually begin until the father was about to die and would then appoint the oldest son to take over. Esau had no interest in this.

Jacob, who was spiritually inclined, and his mother, who favored him, decided to get Esau to transfer his birthright to Jacob. The account states that on a day when Esau was famished, he sold his birthright for some "bread and pottage of lentils" (chap. 25:34).

Peculiar as this transaction may seem to us, it has parallels in ancient documents. In one case, a man by the name of Tupkitilla transferred to his brother his inheritance rights to a grove in exchange for three sheep.[108]

Jacob's questionable means of getting the birthright caused Esau to hate him, and forced Jacob to flee to Haran, where he hoped to find a wife. He arrived there without a dowry. Unlike his father, Isaac, who gained Rebecca for his wife in exchange for much gold and silver (chap. 24:22, 53), Jacob had nothing to offer. In such a case, custom dictated that the future father-in-law and future son-in-law agree on certain services to be rendered by the groom in exchange for a bride. In the case of Jacob, the agreement called for a stiff price of seven years of labor (chap. 29:18).[109] At the end of the seven years, Jacob was the object of deception. Instead of receiving Rachel, the wife he had worked for, he was given the less-desirable older daughter, Leah. His father-in-law, Laban, claimed that the custom of the land dictated that the older one marry first. So Laban exacted of Jacob an additional seven years labor for Rachel. After Jacob served the grasping Laban for a total of twenty years, he decided to leave for home.

Jacob and his family hoped to leave Haran unnoticed and unannounced. This was almost a foolish assumption. Judging by the gift Jacob later sent Esau, he may not only have had a large family assemblage, including wives, children, and servant families, but thousands of head of cattle and other animals (chap. 32:13-15). The account tells us that Jacob had become very wealthy (chap. 30:43).

Several situations connected with Jacob's leaving Haran and his flight to Canaan are borne out archeologically.

Jacob was bound by contract not to mistreat his wives, Laban's daughters, and not to marry other women (chap. 31:50). There are many extant examples of such contracts in ancient Mesopotamian records in which the son-in-law is bound by the father-in-law to specific agreements as part of the marriage contract. In case of failure to fulfill the obligations, a penalty was usually specified.[110]

When Jacob married, both Leah and Rachel

were given attendants, or personal slaves. This practice, too, is well attested in tablets from Mesopotamia.

One reason given by both Rachel and Leah for their willingness to leave their father was that " 'he has reduced our rights to those of foreign women; he sold us, and what he received for us has disappeared' " (verse 15, T.L.B.). The rights of those who were native and legitimate daughters were different from the rights of those who were foreigners or slaves. Native and legitimate children had the highest rights and could not be mistreated. Foreigners or slaves occupied a lower status and had almost no rights.[111]

If Laban treated his daughters as foreigners or slaves, it meant he did not give them their dowry. This seems to be the case here, as implied in the Biblical account. The dowry exacted from Jacob for Rachel and Leah was fourteen years of labor. In addition, Jacob stayed six years longer. The equivalent sum should have been given to the daughters as dowry, which was to be theirs as future security. The dowry was substantially higher if the husband was from another land, as in the case of Jacob, because this was seen as an increased risk. But neither Rachel nor Leah ever received their dowry.

Sons and daughters, even adopted ones, were entitled to inheritance compensations, but Laban's daughters were apparently not counting on this benefit either.

One of the more interesting clarifications archeology makes of the patriarchal account has to do with the incident in which Laban overtook Jacob and expressed what seemed to be one of his greatest concerns: " 'Why did you steal my gods?' " (verse 30, R.S.V.). This account is quite revealing about Laban's religion, and possibly also that of Leah and Rachel, but what would be so important about the disappearance of some inexpensive terra-cotta figurines?

This account, and Laban's concern, puzzled Bible students for many years, but no longer! Tablets found at Nuzi, a town east of the mid-Tigris River, as well as the Code of Hammurabi, have greatly clarified the matter for us.

Each clan had its own protective deity, which was often referred to as "the god of our fathers." They were passed on from generation to generation to whoever inherited the lands. These gods were extremely valuable assets; in case of financial crises they could be pledged as security for a debt.[112] Possession of these gods "ensured the possessor of the family inheritance."[113] It is no wonder that Laban was very anxious for the return of his gods, and Rachel, who had stolen them, was equally anxious to keep them. She stopped short of nothing, as the record indicates, to keep their hiding place secret (verses 34, 35).

Jacob, aware of the great importance of the gods but not knowing that anyone of his group had taken them, declared, " 'Any one with whom you find your gods shall not live' " (verse 32, R.S.V.). Jacob was not being rash; he recognized the seriousness of such a crime, and was aware that Mesopotamian law pronounced the death sentence upon the party guilty of stealing such gods.[114]

Jacob and Laban ended their dispute by coming to terms on a treaty that neither party would cross over the place where a heap of stones and a pillar were erected, to do harm to the other (verses 44-54).

Agreements and treaties were very common in patriarchal times. After an agreement had been drawn up, it would contain the names of a number of witnesses and the name of the scribe. Each witness would place a sign in front of his or her name. After the document was sealed by several persons, it would be in effect.[115]

It used to be that the Bible and Greek writings were the oldest sources of information. Since Greek writings rarely went beyond the fifth century B.C., the Bible stood alone in describing events, customs, and traditions dating back many centuries beyond the Greek accounts. Critics were often severe in their judgments of Biblical accounts. But as more and more information about ancient times is brought to light through archeology, not only does it clarify Scriptures but Scriptures often throw light on texts and other finds of ancient people. Well has Cyrus H. Gordon said, "It is well to remember that the Bible, aside from its great inner worth, remains our leading source for the ancient Near East."[116]

Commenting on the reliability of the patriarchal account, W. F. Albright, dean of Biblical archeologists, points out, "Our case for the substantial historicity of the tradition of the patriarchs is clinched," and then he adds:

> As a whole the picture in Genesis is historical, and

> there is no reason to doubt the general accuracy of the biographical detail and the sketches of personality which makes the patriarchs come alive with a vividness unknown to a single extra-Biblical character in the whole vast literature of the ancient Near East.[117]

It is comforting to know that God's Word is accurate and dependable. Nearly four thousand years of history have not changed this fact. As archeologists bring more and more information to light, those days of so long ago seem to come alive again with an unbelievable clarity.

O God, we thank You for this!

Footnotes

Chapter 1

[1] Sir Leonard Woolley, *Ur of the Chaldees,* p. 14.
[2] Andre Parrot, *Abraham and His Times,* p. 44.
[3] W. F. Albright, "From the Patriarchs to Moses," *Biblical Archeologist,* vol. 36 (1973), p. 42.

Chapter 2

[4] Woolley, *op. cit.,* pp. 168, 169.
[5] Alexander Heidel, *The Babylonian Genesis,* p. 3.
[6] *Ibid.,* p. 64.
[7] Albright, *op. cit.,* pp. 22ff.
[8] S. N. Kramer, *History Begins at Sumer,* p. 184.
[9] H. W. F. Saggs, *Everyday Life in Babylonia and Assyria,* p. 87.
[10] Tikva Frymer-Kensky, "The Atrahasis Epic and Its Significance for Our Understanding of Genesis 1-9," *Biblical Archeologist,* vol. 40 (1977), p. 133. See also p. 147ff.
[11] Edmond Sollenberger, *The Babylonian Legend of the Flood,* p. 27.

Chapter 3

[12] Sir Leonard Woolley, *Excavations at Ur,* p. 59.
[13] *Ibid.,* p. 12.
[14] *Ibid.,* pp. 193, 194.
[15] John B. Curtis and William W. Hallo, "Money and Merchants in Ur III," *Hebrew Union College Annual,* vol. 30 (1959), p. 104.
[16] W. F. Albright, *Archeology, Historical Analogy, and Early Biblical Tradition,* pp. 34, 35.
[17] ———, *The Biblical Period From Abraham to Ezra,* p. 6.
[18] William W. Hallo, *The Ancient Near East,* p. 82.
[19] James L. Kelso, *Archaeology and Our Old Testament Contemporaries,* p. 16.
[20] Albright, *Archeology, Historical Analogy, and Early Biblical Tradition,* p. 34.
[21] Woolley, *Excavations at Ur,* pp. 144, 145.
[22] Parrott, *op. cit.,* p. 19, note 38.
[23] Woolley, *Excavations at Ur,* p. 36.
[24] *Ibid.,* pp. 52ff.

Chapter 4

[25] Kramer, *op. cit.,* p. 11.
[26] ———, *The Sumerians,* p. 241.
[27] ———, *History Begins at Sumer,* p. 9.
[28] *Ibid.*
[29] *Ibid.,* pp. 12-15.
[30] Benno Landsberger, *Three Essays on the Sumerians,* pp. 11, 12.
[31] Georges Roux, *Ancient Iraq,* pp. 158, 159.
[32] S. Jeffrey Wilkerson, "Man's Eighty Centuries in Veracruz," *National Geographic,* vol. 158 (1980), p. 214.
[33] Landsberger, *op. cit.,* p. 14.
[34] Kramer, *The Sumerians,* pp. 140, 142.

[35] Hildegard Lewy, "Anatolia in the Old Assyrian Period," *The Cambridge Ancient History*, Fascicle No. 40 (1965), p. 16.
[36] Landsberger, *op. cit.*, pp. 13, 14.
[37] Kramer, *The Sumerians,* p. 153.
[38] G. E. Wright, *Biblical Archeology* (1960), p. 11.

Chapter 5

[39] H. W. F. Saggs, *The Greatness That Was Babylon,* p. 60.
[40] Wright, *op. cit.* (1957), pp. 40-42.
[41] Albright, "From the Patriarchs to Moses," *Biblical Archeologist,* vol. 36 (1973), pp. 22ff.
[42] Woolley, *Excavations at Ur,* p. 163.
[43] Saggs, *The Greatness That Was Babylon,* p. 58.
[44] Roux, *op. cit.*, p. 164.

Chapter 6

[45] Nelson Glueck, *Rivers in the Desert,* pp. 85, 86.
[46] E. F. Campbell, Jr., ed., *The Biblical Archeologist Reader,* vol. 2 (1957), p. 19.
[47] Woolley, *Excavations at Ur,* p. 32.
[48] Avraham Malamat, "Mari," *Biblical Archeologist,* vol. 34 (1971), p. 8.
[49] *Ibid.*
[50] *Ibid.*, pp. 12-22.

Chapter 7

[51] Parrot, *op. cit.*, p. 41.
[52] Wright, *op. cit.* (1957), pp. 40, 41.
[53] Parrot, *op. cit.*, p. 40.
[54] *Ibid.*, p. 56.
[55] Wright, *op. cit.* (1957), p. 41.
[56] William W. Hallo, "Haran," *Encyclopedia Judaica,* Cecil Roth, ed.
[57] Albright, *Archeology, Historical Analogy, and Early Biblical Tradition,* p. 38.
[58] Wright, *op. cit.* (1957), p. 42.

Chapter 8

[59] Much of the information on Ebla was received by the author by personal interview with Paolo Matthiae, director of the excavation, and Giovanni Pettinato, epigrapher, on the site of Ebla in 1978.
[60] Paolo Matthiae, "Ebla in the Late Early Syrian Period: The Royal Palace and the State Archives," *Biblical Archeologist,* vol. 39 (1976), pp. 94-113.
[61] Parrot, *op. cit.*, pp. 64, 65.
[62] Albright, *Archeology, Historical Analogy, and Early Biblical Tradition,* p. 24.
[63] Kelso, *op. cit.*, pp. 16ff.
[64] Albright, "From the Patriarchs to Moses," *Biblical Archeologist,* vol. 36 (1973), p. 14.

Chapter 9

[65] Roland DeVaux, *Revue Biblique,* vol. 55 (1948), p. 325.

Chapter 10

[66] James B. Pritchard, ed., *The Ancient Near East,* vol. 1, p. 58.
[67] Nelson Glueck, *The River Jordan,* pp. 10, 11.
[68] Saggs, *Everyday Life in Babylonia and Assyria,* p. 36.
[69] Kathleen M. Kenyon, *Amorites and Canaanites,* p. 34.
[70] Avraham Negev, ed., *Archaeological Encyclopaedia of the Holy Land,* p. 105.
[71] John Bright, *A History of Israel,* p. 48.
[72] Wright, *op. cit.* (1960), chapter 1.
[73] James K. West, *Introduction to the Old Testament,* p. 173.

Chapter 11

[74] Freedman, *op. cit.*, vol. 2, pp. 25-28.
[75] Dinah was about as old as Joseph, who turned 17 a few years after this incident, when he was sold into Egypt (Gen. 30:21-25; 37:2).
[76] Wright, *op. cit.* (1957), p. 47.
[77] James L. Kelso, *Perspective,* vol. 13, No. 1 (1972), p. 8.
[78] Negev, *op. cit.*, pp. 17-19.

Chapter 12

[79] W. F. Albright, *Board of American Schools of Oriental Research,* vol. 127 (1952), p. 30.

[80] Bright, *op. cit.*, p. 47.
[81] John Wilson, *The Burden of Egypt*, p. 133.
[82] Bright, *op. cit.*, p. 46.
[83] Wilson, *op. cit.*, p. 134.
[84] I. E. S. Edwards, ed., *The Cambridge Ancient History*, vol. 1, part 2 (1975), p. 501.
[85] Flavius Josephus, *Antiquities of the Jews*, translated by William Whiston, 1. 8. 2.

Chapter 13

[86] Negev, *op. cit.*, p. 141.
[87] Kelso, *Perspective*, vol. 13 (1972), p. 8.
[88] Albright, *Archeology, Historical Analogy, and Early Biblical Tradition*, p. 37.
[89] *Ibid.*, p. 38.
[90] For a discussion of the name Salem, see Albright, "From the Patriarchs to Moses," *Biblical Archeologist*, vol. 36 (1973), pp. 17, 18.
[91] Woolley, *Excavations at Ur*, pp. 144, 145.
[92] Glueck, *Rivers in the Desert*, p. 92.
[93] *Ibid.*
[94] E. A. Speiser, ed. and trans. Genesis., *The Anchor Bible*, p. 164.
[95] Woolley, *Excavations at Ur*, pp. 59, 60, 70, 71.
[96] C. A. Burland, *Peoples of the Sun*, pp. 29, 85.
[97] Albert R. W. Green, *The Role of Human Sacrifice in the Ancient Near East*, p. 149.
[98] Speiser, ed and trans., *Genesis. The Anchor Bible*, p. 171.
[99] Parrot, *op. cit.*, p. 131.

Chapter 14

[100] Much of the information about the present excavations of the cities of the plain was received through interviews on the site with the directors of the excavations, Walter Rast and Tom Schaub.
[101] Glueck, *The River Jordan*, p. 3.
[102] Negev, *op. cit.*, p. 89.
[103] Paul C. Maloney, "Assessing Ebla," *Biblical Archaeology Review* March, 1978, p. 7.
[104] Paolo Matthiae letter to the editor, *Biblical Archeologist*, vol. 43 (1980), p. 133.
[105] Walter Rast and Thomas Schaub, "Bab edh-Dhra," *American School of Oriental Research Newsletter*, No. 8 (1980), pp. 14-17.
[106] Negev, *op. cit.*, p. 89.

Chapter 16

[107] Pritchard, *op. cit.*, p. 169.
[108] Freedman, *op. cit.*, p. 23.
[109] For laws regulating dowries, see Code of Hammurabi, laws 159-161, Pritchard, ed., *op. cit.*, pp. 155, 156.
[110] Freedman, *op. cit.*, pp. 24, 25.
[111] *Ibid.*, p. 27.
[112] Lewy, *op. cit.*, p. 14.
[113] Wright, *op. cit.* (1957), p. 44.
[114] Siegfried H. Horn, *Records of the Past Illuminate the Bible*, p. 24.
[115] For samples of agreements, see Pritchard, *op. cit.*, pp. 168, 169.
[116] Freedman, *op. cit.*, p. 28.
[117] Albright, *The Biblical Period From Abraham to Ezra*, p. 5.

Bibliography

Albright, W. F. *Archeology, Historical Analogy, and Early Biblical Tradition.* Baton Rouge: Louisiana State University Press, 1966.

———. *The Biblical Period From Abraham to Ezra.* New York: Harper and Row, 1963.

———. *Bulletin of American School of Oriental Research*, vol. 127 (1952), p. 30.

———. "From the Patriarchs to Moses," *Biblical Archeologist,* vol. 36, No. 1 (February, 1973), pp. 17ff.

Bright, John. *A History of Israel.* London: SCM Press Ltd., 1959.

Burland, C. A. *Peoples of the Sun.* New York: Praeger Publications, 1976.

Campbell, E. F., Jr., ed. *The Biblical Archeologist Reader,* vol. 2, Missoula, Montana: Scholars Press, 1957.

Curtis, John B., and William W. Hallo. "Money and Merchants in Ur III," *Hebrew College Annual,* vol. 30 (1959), p. 104.

DeVaux, Roland. *Revue Biblique,* vol. 55 (1948), p. 325.

Edwards, I. E. S., ed. *The Cambridge Ancient History,* vol. 1, part 2, third edition. Cambridge, England: Cambridge University Press, 1975.

Freedman, David Noel, ed. *The Biblical Archaeologist Reader,* vol. 2. Missoula, Montana: Scholars Press, 1975.

Frymer-Kensky, Tikva. "The Atrahasis Epic and Its Significance for Our Understanding of Genesis 1-9," *Biblical Archeologist,* vol. 40 (December. 1977), pp. 147ff.

Glueck, Nelson. *The River Jordan.* Philadelphia: Westminster Press, 1946.

———. *Rivers in the Desert.* London: Weidenfeld and Nicolson, 1959.

Green, Albert R. W. *The Role of Human Sacrifice in the Ancient Near East.* Missoula, Montana: Scholars Press, 1975.

Hallo, William W. *The Ancient Near East.* New York: Harcourt Brace, 1971.

———. "Haran," *Encyclopedia Judaica.* Cecil Roth, ed. New York: Macmillan, 1972.

Heidel, Alexander. *The Babylonian Genesis.* Second edition. Chicago: University of Chicago Press, 1963.

Horn, Siegfried H. *Records of the Past Illuminate the Bible.* Washington, D.C.: Review and Herald Publishing Association, 1963.

———. The Spade Confirms the Book (revised edition). Washington, D.C.: Review and Herald Publishing Association, 1980.

Josephus, Flavius. *Antiquities of the Jews.* Trans. by William Whiston. Philadelphia: James B. Smith & Co., 1860.

Kelso, James L. *Archeology and Our Old Testament Contemporaries.* Grand Rapids, Michigan: Zondervan Publishing House, 1966.

———. *Perspective,* vol. 13, No. 1 (Winter, 1972), p. 8.

Kenyon, Kathleen M. *Amorites and Canaanites.* London: Oxford University Press, 1966.

Kramer, S. N. *History Begins at Sumer.* New York: Doubleday Anchor Books, 1959.

———. *The Sumerians.* Chicago: University of Chicago Press, 1963.

Landsberger, Benno. *Three Essays on the Sumerians.* Los Angeles: Undena Publications, 1974.

Lewy, Hildegard. "Anatolia in the Old Assyrian Period," *The Cambridge Ancient History,* Fascicle No. 40. Cambridge, England: Cambridge University Press, 1965.

Malamat Avraham. "Mari," *Biblical Archeologist,* vol. 34, No. 1 (February, 1971), pp. 8, 12-22.

Maloney, Paul C. "Assessing Ebla," *Biblical Archaeology Review*, vol. 4 (March, 1978), p. 7.
Matthiae, Paolo. "Ebla in the Late Early Syrian Period: The Royal Palace and the State Archives," *Biblical Archeologist*, vol. 39 (1976), pp. 94ff.
———. Letter to the editor, *Biblical Archeologist*, vol. 43 (1980), p. 133.
Negev, Avraham, ed. *Archaeological Encyclopaedia of the Holy Land*. Jerusalem: The Jerusalem Publishing House, 1972.
Parrot, Andre. *Abraham and His Times*. Trans. by James H. Farley. Philadelphia: Fortress Press, 1968.
Pritchard, James B., ed. *The Ancient Near East*, vol. 1. Princeton, New Jersey: University of Princeton Press, 1969.
Rast, Walter, and Thomas Schaub. "Bab edh-Dhra," *American School of Oriental Research Newsletter*, No. 8 (June, 1980), pp. 14-17.
Roux, Georges. *Ancient Iraq*. Great Britain: Penguin Books Ltd., 1966.
Saggs, H. W. F. *Everyday Life in Babylonia and Assyria*. New York: G. P. Putnam's Sons, 1967.
———. *The Greatness That Was Babylon*. New York: Hawthorn Books, 1962.
Sollenberger, Edmond. *The Babylonian Legend of the Flood*. London: British Museum, 1966.
Speiser, E. A., ed. and trans. *Genesis. The Anchor Bible*. New York: Doubleday, 1964.
———. *Annual of the American Schools of Oriental Research*, vol. 13 (1932), p. 43.
West, James K. *Introduction to the Old Testament*. New York: Macmillan, 1971.
Wilkerson, S. Jeffrey. "Man's Eighty Centuries in Veracruz," *National Geographic*, vol. 158, No. 2 (August, 1980), p. 214.
Wilson, John A. *The Burden of Egypt*. Chicago: University of Chicago Press, 1951.
Woolley, Sir Leonard. *Excavations at Ur*. London: Ernest Benn Limited, 1955.
———. *Ur of the Chaldees*. New York: Charles Scribner's Sons, 1930.
Wright, G. E. *Biblical Archeology*. Philadelphia: Westminster Press, 1957.
———. *Biblical Archeology*. Abridged edition. Philadelphia: Westminster Press, 1960.